With an
ATTITUDE *of* GRATITUDE

DONALD CHARLES LACY

ATTITUDE *of* GRATITUDE

A PERSONAL/PROFESSIONAL MEMOIR

Providence House Publishers
WWW.PROVIDENCEHOUSE.COM
FRANKLIN, TENNESSEE

Printed in the United States of America

14   13   12   11   10   1   2   3   4   5

Library of Congress Control Number: 2010920635

ISBN: 978-1-57736-431-3

Cover and page design by LeAnna Massingille

PROVIDENCE HOUSE PUBLISHERS
238 Seaboard Lane • Franklin, Tennessee 37067
www.providencehouse.com
800-321-5692

Dedicated to

Anne Marie Lacy
Donna Jean (Lacy) and Terry Beyl
Fillip A. L. Beyl
Sharon Elizabeth Lacy
Martha Elaine (Lacy) and Jeffrey Graham
Natalie Rene Graham
Justin Daniel Graham
Dorothy Marie (Thomas) Lacy

PREFACE

Practice what you preach! Yes, I have urged hundreds of people over the years to be sure to write their autobiographies, but I had not done one—until now.

How would I go about doing a story of my life? At the age of seventy-two I began to ponder not so much what I would say, but how I would say it. What I did not want was a tome of six hundred pages that mostly sat on library shelves in the Midwest and was seldom used. What I also did not want was a listing of facts with a heavy emphasis on genealogy and professional accomplishment.

So, how have I decided to tell my story or, at least, some of it? It seemed to me the wisest and most practical method would be simply to take a year, and to each day deal with the *past, present,* and *future.* I determined *during my seventy-fifth year* I would do just that; so, I spent 2008 writing everyday in notebooks my thoughts and feelings.

My purpose in the style was twofold: 1. *Readability.* I sought to write in the language of the general public and neither for those in academia nor in theology. I want everyone who is interested to read this work without using an accompanying reference book. I do not want professionalism to be a barrier. 2. *Transparency.* Who is this guy anyway? We know about him, but we really don't know him. For that reason, you will discover both head and heart at work. You will find the mixing of the past, present, and future in ways that may be unexpected. It is a book of honesty and sincerity.

This volume does not in any way seek to record my extensive literary and ecumenical ministries. That may come at another day and time. These areas provide books within themselves and cover virtually a fifty-year period.

I am grateful for the help received from three of my aunts in regard to genealogical information: Mrs. Marjorie (Lacy) Luellen, Mrs. Patty (Lacy) Keesling, and Mrs. Marjorie (Everett) Walradth.

The People of Praise and Melissa M. Hathaway were instrumental in providing this manuscript. To them I say, "Thank you."

Now, "with an attitude of gratitude," which has long been my philosophy of life, I hope you will find these pages both enjoyable and insightful.

D. C. L.

Donald Charles Lacy, six months

Lacy at seventeen years old

Lacy and Dorothy in front of their first parsonage at Philadelphia UMC in 1959

Lacy's daughter Donna Jean, her husband, Terry Beyl, and their son, Fillip A. L. Beyl

Lacy at forty years old

Lacy's daughter Martha Elaine, her husband, Jeffery Graham, and their children, Justin Daniel and Natalie Rene

Lacy at fifty-five years old

Lacy's wife, Dorothy Marie (Thomas) Lacy

Lacy's daughter Sharon Elizabeth Lacy

Lacy at seventy-five years old

Lacy's daughter Anne Marie Lacy

With an
ATTITUDE *of* GRATITUDE

JANUARY
2 0 0 8

TUESDAY, JANUARY 1ST

Lord God, Lamb of God, Who takes away the sins of the world, thank You for a new and promising year!

Grant Your will be done and Your ways prevail in all of our lives. We beg of You always to grant Your Holy Spirit.

New opportunities are open to us and potentiality for good is all about us. Come Holy Spirit with Your guiding presence.

I rededicate myself to Christ and His Church. I seek to fulfill my destiny in this world in hope of everlasting life.

I give thanks for everyone and everything. My Savior, Jesus the Christ, lives for me and dies for me. Hallelujah!

WEDNESDAY, JANUARY 2ND

Another precious day of the new year has dawned. As usual, I read from *My Utmost For His Highest* by Oswald Chambers, along with other materials.

A long-standing habit of intercessory prayer and holy communion gave me an open but fortifying spirit for the day.

We attended a breakfast for United Methodist retired pastors and their wives (spouses). It was mostly good news with a little bad news. Just being together and sharing our "war stories" was worthwhile, but why does there continue to be alienation among us? Perhaps it is our competitive nature. It seems we have yet fully to learn that forgiveness and reconciliation are essentials for those who profess the Faith, especially the clergy.

My own life has often fallen short of Saint Paul's "Love Chapter." Yes, "Love is patient and kind; it is not jealous or boastful . . ." We must wait for heaven fully to perfect us.

We belong to You, Lord, and on our knees we seek to be the best people we can be under the inspiration of the Holy Spirit.

THURSDAY, JANUARY 3RD

How magnificent are Your ways, Lord! Our puny minds and lukewarm hearts struggle to understand You.

A long-standing habit of reading papers and sipping coffee early in the morning in a favorite restaurant is a joy. It is a moment of the morning I cherish.

For many years, I have read *The Indianapolis Star* to give me news from the state and beyond. The paper is no longer what it once was!

Time for my wife and me to shop in Indianapolis and Carmel. Then, an evening of food and fellowship with our daughter Sharon was enjoyed.

Our television seemed to be on fire with news from the Iowa caucus. Dear Lord, please give us a president who knows You and will follow You.

FRIDAY, JANUARY 4TH

Today, I awake giving thanks for my seventy-fifth birthday. I have never known when the presence of the living God has been absent from my life.

My younger brother, Mike, treated me to a sumptuous breakfast. We are very different in personality. He is a good brother.

Time of seclusion and much reflection, wondering how much longer God will enable me to live in this world. Trusting this autobiographical sketch will be a blessing.

Grandson Fillip called and sang "Happy Birthday" to me. His grandfather hopes and prays he will be the finest of men for his time.

My wife took me to dinner and we shared our lives, now more than forty-eight years of marriage. Some difficult years, but lots of love!

SATURDAY, JANUARY 5TH

Greeted the morning about 5:00 AM, which is customary, and gave thanks for God's goodness. Feeling confident and ready to move ahead.

When I was a little boy, my mother, Marian (Walradth) Lacy, and my father, Charles William Lacy, showed me where I was born. My birthplace was in Stoney Creek Township of Henry County, Indiana, out in the country near the town of Blountsville. At the time, the town had well more than two hundred people in it. There was a school at the north edge, which had the first through the eighth grades. I was a student there until near the end of the sixth grade. Eldon Holcomb and Max Stanley were favorite boyhood friends. We lived in, at least, five different rentals there. My father worked in a factory in Muncie. During these years, my parents became professing Christians.

What years are most precious to a person's life? I don't have an answer to that, but I can say without hesitation that all of them have been good, but some were better than others.

In the late 1930s and early 1940s, Blountsville was a bustling little town. It was largely self-sufficient with a grain elevator, service station and garage, grocery store, restaurant, stockyard, school, churches, insurance agency, post office, general store, blacksmith shop, train depot, barbershop, and hardware store. Briefly, there was also both a car dealership and a physician.

Blountsville was not unique with its many services. This was also true of towns close by, such as Mooreland and Losantville.

SUNDAY, JANUARY 6TH

Glory be to the Father, Son, and Holy Spirit! Another opportunity for congregational worship is at hand. Thank You, Lord Jesus.

Worshipped at College Avenue UMC in Muncie, Indiana. The brief sermon was splendidly done. Holy Communion was meaningful. Greeted old friends Ralph and Betty Bushey. He was very supportive during my time as associate pastor there from 1964 to 1966. Ralph is a retired school administrator.

Reflected on last Sunday's guest preaching that I did at Saint Andrew Presbyterian in Muncie. The theme was the "Call to Be One." The congregation was attentive and certainly respectful.

For most of my pastoral career, I have believed the "call to be one," especially from Saint John's 17th chapter, but not limited to it, should be preached with some frequency. Christian unity is never an option; it is always an imperative.

I have never been one for New Year's resolutions, so I have not counted the days into the new year and recorded my progress!

MONDAY, JANUARY 7TH

I sense Your presence, O Lord. I love Your Kingdom. You know all about everyone. Nevertheless, I must pray at length for others and myself.

Our Conference Christian Unity Committee met in Kokomo, Indiana. Praise God! It was a time of serious interest and brotherly sharing.

Only God knows how many hours I have spent in ecumenical and interreligious ministry. It has been and is a calling I must never deny. I am very grateful for the hundreds, perhaps thousands, of people I have met in this long ministry. They have greatly enriched my life. It has taken me to many states and cities.

From time to time, we can know the will of God with certainty. Of course, we must never brag about it!

You have given me so much, Lord. Please make me always grateful and generous. When I am arrogant for whatever reason, please forgive me.

TUESDAY, JANUARY 8TH

Dear God, I overslept this morning! No time was left for normal prayers and Eucharist. Sorry, Lord, I promise to do better.

Finished my regular column for *The Star Press* (Muncie, Indiana). It is a promotional piece for the Week of Prayer for Christian Unity, (January 18–25) a long-standing emphasis of mine.

Reflected on an Ecumenical Happening in April of 1978 at Seymour, Indiana First UMC, where I was pastor from 1974 to 1979. Everyone in the state was invited and we put much effort into it. UMC Bishop of Indiana Ralph T. Alton preached over local TV, workshops were provided by national leaders, and dinner was served. The special day was concluded with a service of Holy Communion. Dr. Charles L. Hutchinson and I were the celebrants. It may not have been an historic occasion, but it certainly was stupendous!

I have always enjoyed giving away copies of my books and have done so countless times. Of course, at some point, you do have to sell some!

During my Walkerton, Indiana UMC years (1993 to 1999), Al's Diner on Koontz Lake was a favorite regular meeting place for our two men's breakfast groups. Altogether, this ministry involved about thirty fellows.

WEDNESDAY, JANUARY 9TH

Awoke with resolve to do my normal readings prayers, and Holy Communion. The Holy Spirit abides and provides.

Prepared for Rotary Club meeting, plus the board business afterward, in New Castle, Indiana. Congressman Mike Pence spoke briefly to us.

Over these many years, I have enjoyed membership in service clubs across the state. Besides Rotary, there were Kiwanis, Lions (president), and Optimists.

Dorothy and I motored to Winchester, Indiana to get her Buick serviced. While there, we also delighted in chicken dinners.

The mysteries of life and death appear even more so in later life. Not knowing one's future abode is frightening, until we appropriate our Faith and accept death as expectant sons and daughters of the King.

THURSDAY, JANUARY 10TH

O Lord, what a gratifying time of worship with You! I know You listen carefully to the dozens of precious persons lifted up to You.

Coffee and *The Indianapolis Star* with conversation made the stop worthwhile at Mac's in Muncie. George Harris, a Centerite greeted me; we were in high school at the same time.

A happy time of correspondence gave me much satisfaction, even peace of mind. Special was the letter I sent to Emma Jane Hostetler in Walkerton, Indiana.

Visited with Jeff Snider at the Muncie downtown post office and told him he should run for mayor. He is very good with the public.

A Rotary district meeting in Hagerstown, Indiana brought back memories, mostly good ones. I was the UMC pastor there (1966 to 1970).

FRIDAY, JANUARY 11TH

Prayer, indeed, breathes life into one's soul. What is more privileged than to converse with God on your knees?

A time of contacting libraries in the Indianapolis metro area brought a sense of successful outreach. O my, the potential!

Sought to bring some loose ends together. I must stay focused on these later years of ministry. The Lord will provide.

I remember my nearly fifty years of pastoral appointments with deep respect and appreciation. Really, there were no bad appointments!

Now and forever, God works His will and ways through us. Is this predestination? I am not smart enough to know that answer.

SATURDAY, JANUARY 12TH

O Lord, Your powers are so awesome! Thank You for enabling me to pray more spontaneously. Yes, Lord, we have no secrets from you.

Sifted and sorted material for the next mailing to my Associates—LIFE (Lacy Institute For Ecumenism). Significant work! Brought the advisory council up-to-date for expenses in 2007. Ran a deficit again, but this was expected. The council is composed of Gary Reif (American Baptist), Mark Eutsler (UMC), Barry Wampler (UMC), and Father Dennis Goth (Roman Catholic). Very grateful for their interest.

Turf wars in the parish ministry can be more than just a ripple on the water. They can be fierce and long-lasting! However, our God is merciful and forgiving. I do believe some of these such wars are born from clergy, who sense a strong responsibility for their flock, and that is commendable.

Who knows more about people's lives in a community than the parish pastors? If we have been at the same charge for some years, I doubt anyone does.

As has been my custom for a few years, I did a late intercessory prayer and Holy Communion for a precious person. Then, I regularly send a copy of the service to each of them as a kind of spiritual memento. Their number is now in the hundreds.

SUNDAY, JANUARY 13TH

Praise be to God the Father, the Son, and the Holy Spirit. Our God is one in three and three in one—the Holy Trinity.

We worshipped at Fishers UMC, near Indianapolis. It was a traditional service that flowed with obvious freedom.

It was our day to sit with our grandchildren Natalie Rene and Justin Daniel. Our daughter Martha and her husband, Jeffrey Graham, are their parents. This grandfather labors sometimes (really often) to communicate and relate to them, but he loves them dearly. I pray for them everyday.

My grandparents were a major influence in my life from the beginning. They were Glade and Grace (Gibson) Walradth and Guy and Christie (McCall) Lacy.

O Lord, call us to be grateful for those who have given so much to us and now are gone from sight.

MONDAY, JANUARY 14TH

Dear Lord, please supply all of my needs, including those of which I am unaware, except as You reveal them. I yield myself to You.

Surveyed the numerous United Methodist pastors with Indiana connections I have known with special respect. They were: Gail Davis, John R. Dicken, Russell Fenstermacher, and Edwin Helm.

Added to them would be: Susan Messenger, A. Wesley Pugh, David H. Tripp, James B. Willyard, Ron Bowman, Wes Brookshire, Norm Glassburn, Al Kundenreich, John Pattison, and Forrest Bowers.

Some others were: R. Larry Smith, Ron VerLee, David Heim, James McDonald, Chris Roberts, Keith Olson, John Wortinger, Steve Beach, Lamar Imes, Alda Carter, and Lemuel Johnson.

And I must not forget: Jim Beckley, Gary L. Forbes, Scott Shoaff, Charles I. Johnson, John E. Weeks, John R. Parks, Wayne Yeater, Ed McClarnon, Byron Stroh, Gary Phillips, and Jack Hartman.

TUESDAY, JANUARY 15TH

Morning worship of prayers, Scripture, and Holy Communion somewhat disrupted for various reasons. Of course, God understands!

Wrote personal letters to Donna and Terry Beyl, my daughter and son-in-law. They are caring professionals and good to me on my birthday.

Wrote to grandson Fillip A. L. Beyl and thanked him for my birthday gifts. One was a delightful picture of us together.

Received a thank you from the Rev. John R. Parks for a gift I made to Hartford City Grace UMC in honor of his ministry. John is a solid, low-key pastor.

Television was blaring out the returns of the Michigan primary. Mitt Romney was the clear winner among Republicans. He is a polished, handsome fellow.

WEDNESDAY, JANUARY 16TH

What is better than pouring out your heart to the living God? Well, not much, my friends! His powerful presence offers perpetual salvation.

Must continue my listing of UMC pastors with Indiana connections I have known with special respect. They were: Rex Charles, Don Carpenter, Howard Wright, Mark L. Dicken, Gary Schaar, and Leon Nicholson.

Others to be included were: Charles Ballard, Robert W. Koenig, Charles Armstrong, Myron Yonker, John Wantz, John Gaus, Richard Hamilton, Bob DeLong, Earl Stanley McKee, George Millard, and Boyde Nelson.

Then, there were: Guy Ramsey, Ross Vandine, Floyd Cook, Lyle Rasmussen, Max Case, Robert L. Epps, Allan Wilson, Charles Gipson, Ken Holtzkom, Cliff Carmichael, and Gregg Rittenhouse.

Finally, worthy of mention were: Larry Ray, Frank Beard, David Maish, Robert Holmes, Dan Motto, Harold Bachert, Foster Williams, Jay Althouse, Ralph Karstedt, Newman Jeffrey, and Tom Kuhn.

THURSDAY, JANUARY 17TH

Father, all glorious Father, all victorious for the living of these days. Your love, mercy, forgiveness, and strength, O Lord, are always needed.

"Have no anxiety about anything but by prayer and pleading with thanksgiving, let your requests be made known to God." How magnificently and powerfully Saint Paul puts it!

While I have never been one saturated in genealogy, it is helpful to have some facts. For example, the father and mother of my grandfather Guy Charles Lacy were William and Alice (Himes) Lacy. Grandfather Lacy had one sister (Myrtle) and three brothers (Elmer W., Benjamin, and Loyd). Their lives were mostly lived in Henry and Delaware counties, Indiana.

Dorothy provided an appetizing meatloaf for dinner. What an excellent cook she has been all these years. I love her so much.

Please give us Your signs, Lord, during these difficult and trying times. Our need is especially for mysterious and yet concrete indication of Your love, power, and mercy.

FRIDAY, JANUARY 18TH

Dear God, the only great One of the universe, You are waiting for me to come to You! I do so humbly, sincerely, confidently, and honestly.

Grandmother Christie Marie (McCall) had four sisters (Lena, Bertha, Pearl, and Jeanette). She also had six brothers (Cleo, Marion, George, Wilbur, Wayne, and Charles Jr.). Her parents were Charles S. and Mertie Ann (Bridget) McCall. Their lives and children were mostly spent in and around New Castle, Indiana.

Went to Chamber of Commerce meeting in New Castle. Chamber provided a time of information on the legislature. Valuable.

Watched a Charles Bronson movie on TV. It was part of the Death Wish series. Entertaining and, from one viewpoint, spiritually significant.

How beautiful, dear Lord, it is to find You among people we have never met before. The unforeseen circumstances You bring into our lives continue to surprise and amaze me!

SATURDAY, JANUARY 19TH

Lord Jesus, I need more endurance and sacrificial spirit. I must not dote on my retirement good fortune.

Perused manuscripts that were years old for possible publication. Not sure where that leads, but God knows and what else matters?

I gave some thought to a telephone conversation I had with Aunt Marjorie Walradth. She misses my Uncle Buss (Verl). I had his funeral a few weeks ago.

Give me strength and patience, O Lord, for everything and everyone. I have often failed, sometimes dismally, in the virtue of patience.

Walked in the Muncie Mall, which was invigorating. Lord, keep me sensitive in regard to my health and habits.

SUNDAY, JANUARY 20TH

Precious Lord, hold my hand; lead me on and let me stand. How touching some of the hymns are that come from my upbringing!

From my earliest recollection, my father and mother were Christian people. They came from a revivalist era, but were not anti-Catholic.

Dorothy and I worshipped at Yorktown UMC. It was our final full-time appointment and we still prize those good folks.

The Christian Unity Service at Grade Episcopal Church in Muncie was vital. There was excellent participation and a joyous spirit.

I visited with a Catholic friend Louisa Reese, who had given me some-time ago a gift book, *My Daily Eucharist*, which is very helpful.

MONDAY, JANUARY 21ST

How sweet and comforting it is to visit with Jesus, our Master and Brother! How do others live their lives without Him?

Much aware it is Martin Luther King Jr.'s Day. The media did some uplifting and positive things.

I worked in my recently published materials files, so additions can be placed with the Indiana Historical Society. It has my most complete collection.

My grandfather Charles Gladstone Walradth only used the first name of "Glade." His father and mother were Eli Warner Walradt and Viretta Ellen (Wisehart) Walradt ("h" added early in twentieth century). Grandfather Walradth had two brothers (Merrill E. and J. Lloyd) and two sisters (Margaret Olive Grace and Hasel Clair).

The powers of darkness sometimes come with the force of a night without light of any kind. Your Holy Scriptures have told us this would be so. Remind us of their ongoing imperative relevance.

TUESDAY, JANUARY 22ND

Praise God from Whom all blessings flow! Help us, Lord, to recognize the multiple blessings showered upon us.

Our youngest daughter, Martha Elaine, was born forty-one years ago on this date. What a lovely and committed wife and mother she now is! When I was pastor of First UMC in Hagerstown, Indiana, she was born on Sunday morning at 9:00 AM. She weighed just over nine pounds. I had taken Dorothy to the Reid Memorial Hospital in Richmond, Indiana for delivery. Then I returned to the church to conduct worship. The hospital called just before the service began and told me. When I made the announcement to the congregation, they were filled with joy!

I believe our private schools at all levels are doing a better job of educating our students than tax-supported schools. Evangelical and Roman Catholic institutions overall are making a solid contribution both academically and morally.

Have professional sports and their relationship to television produced a monstrous problem for our society? I don't have the wisdom to determine that, but I tend to think so.

Always loved to visit and purchase materials at the Daughters of Saint Paul bookstore in downtown Chicago.

WEDNESDAY, JANUARY 23RD

Do not judge others and God will not judge you; do not condemn others and God will not condemn you; forgive others and God will forgive you. My how our dear Lord has a way of placing a mirror, so we can see ourselves the way we really are. Some days it ain't pretty!

Ninety-four years ago, my mother, Marian Marcile Walradth, was born to Glade and Grace (Gibson) Walradth in Delaware County, Indiana. She was their first child. My mother was a strikingly beautiful young woman. In fact, as a teenager, she did some modeling.

Rotary meeting was filled with interest and fellowship. Judge Bob Witham of New Castle was the guest speaker.

I love Your Kingdom, Lord, and in a way I have loved it even before I recognized that awesome reality!

O dear God, keep giving us Your salvation in ways that alter and sometimes completely change our lives. Thank You.

THURSDAY, JANUARY 24TH

Thank You, Lord, for motivating me at times into praying for dozens and dozens of Your precious souls. It is a noble and much needed work!

Continued to labor in getting ready to take materials to Indiana Historical Society. It is very important they are safely placed before my death.

When we take the long view of life, everything changes from the moment to eternity. I have most of seventy-five years to give an accounting.

Called to northeast Indianapolis, near Broad Ripple, to give a keynote address to a group associated with the Focolare Movement (international Catholic Unity group). Their focus is on the Blessed Virgin Mary and Christian Unity. I dealt with both and this seemed to resonate with everyone. They were kind, appreciative, and very interested. Holy Spirit much present!

During my pastorate at Meadowdale UMC (1981–1985), now Northwest, in Indianapolis, I grew in my ability to counsel people. Having worked under Foster Williams, I was able to minister to my own clientele. It was the development of a dimension of my professional/personal life that gave me great satisfaction and uncovered skills I was unaware I possessed.

FRIDAY, JANUARY 25TH

Dear God, Your miracles are all about us, but sometimes we who profess Your Son's name are fearful and probably rightfully so.

Totaled book signings for 2006 and 2007. Those for 2007 were an amazing number, almost seventy! Many good folks working in these stores.

Recalled the Palm Sunday evening I preached at Van Buren UMC (Indiana) in April of 1965. Tornadoes were coming through Indiana and people were being killed. Pastor John R. Parks and I finished the service by candlelight. We thought the stained glass windows might come down on the congregation. I drove back to Muncie through some vicious weather and didn't realize the extreme severity of what was happening until the next morning.

Sermon talkbacks are helpful and fruitful, provided the pastor handles them well and the laity is responsive. If there is real rapport between him and the laity, much can be learned. It is an excellent way to put the pastor in touch with the day-to-day needs of the congregation.

Detached concern is an inadequate but helpful way of helping us to understand our role as pastors in critical and gut-wrenching situations that become very emotional. God understands!

SATURDAY, JANUARY 26TH

How graciously present You are, O Lord! To think the Supreme Being of the universe would condescend even to me is more than awesome.

Relished some leisurely reading in various publications, including my new *2008 World Almanac*. How much time have I spent reading in my lifetime?

Gave thanks for four very helpful lay leaders over the years—Pete Mann (Philadelphia UMC); Tom Johnson (Seymour First UMC); Dave Parkison (Yorktown UMC); and Dick Reese (Walkerton UMC).

The most powerfully spiritual events with thousands present I remember experiencing had to do with the Promise Keepers, one in Indianapolis and another in Atlanta.

Gave thanks for Dorothy's reasonably good health. When we lived in Hebron, Indiana, serving Salem Community UMC, she almost died.

SUNDAY, JANUARY 27TH

Ask and you will receive; seek and you will find; knock and the door will be opened to you. Yes, Lord, I hear You!

Dorothy and I worshipped at First UMC in Anderson, Indiana. It was and is one of those churches marked "status," but we found it much alive and with solid ministry.

During my pastorate at First UMC Hagerstown (1966–1970), I tried to set up nationally known speakers to aid the church out of some parochial ways. Among those were: Byron Stroh (North UMC, Indianapolis); John W. Fisher (Ball Corporation, Muncie); Ozzie Pruett (First Baptist, Indianapolis); and Ronald E. Osborn (Christian Theological Seminary, Indianapolis). During the same pastorate, I saw Superintendent of Schools Robert Clark through his ordeal with cancer. When he died, his wife called me to his bedside in the Henry County Memorial Hospital at 2:00 AM in the morning.

Were there forces in my denomination that would like to have driven me out of the ordained ministry or, at least, made me change denominations? Yes, but I never gave them any justifiable reason because I was morally sound and was never guilty of maladministration. The Holy Spirit abided, provided, and guided!

Yes, "whether we live or die, we belong to the Lord." For what else can we ask?

MONDAY, JANUARY 28TH

How close You are, O Lord, how close You are! Sometimes we are carried into a land where life and death are essentially the same.

Learned that Aunt Erma (Lacy) Kleihauer had passed away. She was past ninety years of age. She was a registered nurse, graduating from the Ball State nursing program in the late 1930s. We corresponded for years. She was always wise and affirming. She will be missed. Her husband, Hopkins (UMC pastor in the Chicago area), was a major influence in my life. As a teenager, he showed me there could be a lot more to religion than the fundamentalism of east central Indiana!

Reeders Heating and Air Conditioning came and repaired our furnace. They relieved us of a serious potential problem.

Delivered materials to the Indiana Historical Society. Eric Mundell graciously received them and we chatted for a moment.

While I am an outsider to the workings of higher education, it does seem to me the expenditure of money has gone beyond our ability as tax payers to handle it. Whatever happened to sacrifice? Perhaps we have redefined the word!

TUESDAY, JANUARY 29TH

Genuine prayer always has the characteristics of sincerity, humility, and honesty. Good to keep this in our memory banks!

We went to Fishers to sit with Martha and Jeff's little boy, Justin Daniel. It was a moment for mother Martha to take Natalie for play time. When they returned, Natalie wanted her grandfather to play with her and I did. Maybe I can do the very important grandfatherly thing after all. Hope so!

In a general way, a certain sense of completion has now come over me and my life. While I would like to know what that means, I freely admit this is first and foremost God's business.

Donna (Lacy) Beyl arrived home to Fishers from Oakland, California. The weather was unsettled and stormy, so I was relieved and gave thanks.

Loved deeply the Maundy Thursday services in the various churches I pastored and the spiritual depths provided by receiving Holy Communion. Often the power of the Holy Spirit was more evident to me than during the Good Friday and Easter services. To receive His Body and Blood touched the deeper levels of my soul and I was very grateful. It was as though I had tasted firsthand and personally the glorious gift of salvation.

WEDNESDAY, JANUARY 30TH

Thank You, Lord, for prodding me into an ever-increasing prayer life. Indeed, prayer is life and life is prayer! I owe so much to those who have prayed for me, both the church militant and triumphant.

This is the birthday of my brother Joseph Allen Lacy. He would have been sixty-nine today. Joe was a career officer in the U.S. Army. Prior to going to the service at the age of eighteen, he tended to be an unruly young man. During his military experience, he developed his considerable talents. No one could question his patriotism and military commitment. He flew helicopters in Vietnam.

Our Rotary Club was thrilled by groups from the Choral Department of New Castle High School. Our club is pleased and proud to be a sponsor.

I am reminded this is also President Franklin Delano Roosevelt's birthday. He was my first political idol. Remember his death in April of 1945 quite well. The somber scenes that followed I will likely never forget. While we were near the end of World War II, he did not live to witness the celebrations and gratitude of the America people and her allies.

We Christians are called to love one another. It is that simple and yet that difficult. My experience is that if we try to do it within our own power, we shall surely fail.

THURSDAY, JANUARY 31ST

O Lord, thank You for Your love, mercy, and forgiveness. Your goodness is far above and beyond mine.

Reflected on probably the most loyal friend I ever had in the churches. His name was Norman Rusch and the appointment was Indianapolis Union Chapel UMC, near Keystone at the Crossing. He treated me like a son and called me even after I left there to see how I was doing. Others there come to mind who were supportive: Maida Dawson, Gene Butler, Laura Hicks, Ed Arens, Donna Stuart (church secretary), Tom and Pansy Tucker, Bill Bastian, Ray Taylor, Miles and Bess Plzak, Dale Trinkle, and Oscar Sering. I was there from 1970 to 1973. My two immediate predecessors had been there a total of less than three years combined! It was a time of rapid statistical growth for the people, but with serious problems that had been there for many years.

Fascinated by the heroics of the First Century Christians. Those men and women were so convinced of their Savior and Lord's saving power they were willing to lay down their lives for Him. Others who followed over the centuries are also to be greatly honored. They make us fall to our knees in shame! Perhaps some of us will be called to give our lives for Christ and His Church!

From time to time, I admire our daughters' (Donna and Martha) wedding pictures. They were and are so inspirationally beautiful. Thankfully, they married gifted and caring men.

Who can say whether Rush Limbaugh is helpful or detrimental? While he can cause love/hate emotions that seem to reach beyond common sense, he needs to be seen simply as another voice exercising free speech.

FEBRUARY
2 0 0 8

FRIDAY, FEBRUARY 1ST

When morning guilds the skies, my heart awakening cries; may Jesus Christ be praised! This must be the best of all ways to start our days.

A light snow with some ice and sleet made for treacherous driving. Of course, that did not keep me from going out for coffee and reading *The Indianapolis Star.*

Research in my study brought to mind with deep appreciation key professors I had at Christian Theological Seminary for my master of divinity degree (1961). Ronald E. Osborn (church history), Walter W. Sikes (philosophy), George C. Stuart (preaching), and Joseph Smith (world religions) were standouts. They helped to give me a theological grounding that served me well all of my adult life. They were gentlemen and scholars of the highest order.

Innumerable times I have felt the Holy Spirit presided over the worship services in churches to which I was appointed.

My letter from Robert F. Kennedy (1966), which appears in my *Collected Works,* has been a conversational piece for many.

SATURDAY, FEBRUARY 2ND

You know what we are going to say, O Lord, before we say it! Nevertheless, we must pour out our hearts!

A day of ongoing pursuing of personal and professional effects. Thank God, I saved as much as I did over the years.

Relished in delight the days of my doctor of ministry program from 1974 to 1976 at Christian Theological Seminary. Great experience! Key professors were Keith Watkins in preaching, Charles Ashanin in Orthodox theology, and Clark Williamson in Jewish/Christian relations. Each strengthened me in both my professional and personal life. My doctoral project was "Preaching as a Lay/Clergy Event." It sought to bring preaching in contact with the living concerns of people's lives. It required cooperation of lay officers of First UMC in Seymour, Indiana.

Only a few people ever cared about the knowledge I possessed. Many cared about the way I affirmed them and their lives.

I believe one of the greatest needs today among young women, married or single, is to know an older man (father figure) that respects them and expects no favors. He should provide conversation and affirmation.

SUNDAY, FEBRUARY 3RD

Read papers and drank coffee at Mac's Restaurant. Profitable conversations made it a special stop. Another learning experience!

Dorothy and I worshipped at Saint Andrew Presbyterian. Youth provided leadership and pastor celebrated Holy Communion.

After we ate our delicious meal at Texas Steakhouse, I worked in my study. Trust the Holy Spirit to write this autobiography.

We spent the evening watching the Super Bowl. New York Giants upset New England Patriots. Wow, what a game!

Gave thanks for Mark Jacobs, who has been virtually indispensable for me, at Providence House Publishers.

MONDAY, FEBRUARY 4TH

My prayer life is shifting some again. The dear Lord does not always fit into my well-worn categories!

Learned again that going through a vast amount of materials can be hard work, but rewarding. For example, while at Leesburg UMC (1987–1990), some of my best journaling was done there. The year of 1989, in particular, was significant.

A major impact on my life in my twenties was Bishop Fulton J. Sheen. He was a genius on television and his popular books were just what I needed. His books: *Way to Inner Peace* (1954), *God Loves You* (1955), *The*

Power of Love (1964), and *Walk with God* (1965) were formative. His ideas even found their way into some of my very early sermons. His wisdom transcended a rigid Roman Catholicism.

The Old Order Amish are favorite folks. Even though they may seem strange to some, their witness is unique and much needed.

I have some excellent church treasurers, who took care of my needs over the years. Certainly Dick Groves (Yorktown UMC) was one of them.

TUESDAY, FEBRUARY 5TH

Must stay busy but always in harmony with the Holy Spirit. That takes some moving of obstructions and barricades!

Having some feelings of gentle emptiness. My Savior and Lord knows how difficult it is for me to be patient about much of anything.

The difference between headlong, personal, and/or professional ambition and being motivated in faith with God-given guidelines and goals can be like night and day.

Thank You, Jesus, for my United Methodist brothers in the ordained ministry. Please strengthen those under heavy temptation and who are seriously discouraged.

The United Methodist Church has given me much, both spiritually and materially. Praise God from Whom all blessings flow.

WEDNESDAY, FEBRUARY 6TH

I love Your Kingdom, Lord. Where else can I go and not jeopardize my eternal soul? Praise be to You now and forevermore.

Much interested in the Super Tuesday primaries. *USA Today* confirmed McCain's ascendancy and Obama/Clinton deadlock.

Lively Rotary meeting in New Castle. New Mayor James Small (faithful Anglican) was our speaker. Impressive fellow! We gave him a standing ovation.

Recalled Paul E. Ingels and Wendy Ward of *The Palladium-Item* (Richmond, Indiana), who did feature stories on my literary ministry.

Likewise, recalled Brian Blair of *The Republic* in Columbus, Indiana, who did an extensive story on my *Collected Works*.

THURSDAY, FEBRUARY 7TH

Precious moments of prayer given in persistence must be our most powerful of all exercises. More patience, Lord!

God bless the bookstore folks, who have aided me in the distribution of my published material. I asked for help and the Lord sent it! Those who immediately come to mind are Sarah Billings, Linda Keller, John Moore, Ronda Grunemann, and Michelle Grenat (Barnes and Noble); Scott Neal and Cheryl Sawyer (Family Christian Stores); John Thompson (Borders); Peggy McCarty (Open Door Bookstore); and Daryl Mosley (Books-A-Million). There are many others and I do appreciate them so very much. I pray with thanksgiving for them frequently.

Thank You, Lord, for this literary ministry that has again begun to thrive. The credit goes to You.

There is a real art to pastoral hospital visits. We must be aware of the needs of the patient, family, friends, and hospital staff. More than some clergy seem to realize we do represent Christ and His Church.

Holding divergent and tension-filled parts of our lives together in meaningful creativity is indeed the work of the Holy Spirit.

FRIDAY, FEBRUARY 8TH

Heavenly Father, the Church Universal for centuries has utilized Lent as a special time to prepare for Christ's crucifixion and resurrection. Keep us ever humble.

Sometimes in the life of the churches, certain people make their pastors appear better and more competent than they are. It is a gift of service and love.

One such person was our organist at Yorktown UMC. His name was Darrell Hughes. He was the son of a prominent Nazarene pastor. Whether it be Sunday morning services, weddings or funerals, he made me look good! His mother, Naydine, often visited our services and praised my sermons. One Sunday, she told me with a sly grin, "You are almost good enough to be a Nazarene!" Some years later, I had her celebrative funeral.

A great theologian/philosopher of our time and perhaps for all time is Thomas Merton. His voluminous writings will likely inspire generations.

When I am tempted to drop into complaining and exaggerating problems, I begin writing thank-you notes. It is a worthy pursuit I have practiced for many years.

SATURDAY, FEBRUARY 9TH

Jesus loves me, this I know, for the Bible tells me so. Well, friends, that is pretty hard to improve upon.

Having grandchildren has developed a new dimension in my life. It has drawn me closer to all children and I consider that a very good thing. To become Christlike is to become childlike. For some of us, intellectually and academically oriented, this is hard to learn . . . and accept!

Therese Weakland and Louisa Reese at Saint Mary (Muncie) have been wonderful friends for some years now. They have continually affirmed my ecumenism. Louisa has done feature columns on my work for *The Catholic Moment*, official newspaper of the Diocese of Lafayette in Indiana. Father Thomas C. Widner and Greg A. Otolski of *The Criterion*, official newspaper of the Indianapolis Archdiocese, have been good to run major columns I have written on the Blessed Virgin Mary.

Pastors, like many I suppose, can be overqualified, underemployed, and underpaid! There is comfort in knowing God can put all the pieces together.

Funeral services are major moments for doing lasting ministry. For thirty minutes or so a pastor has a singular opportunity that may never return. Thank God for those moments!

SUNDAY, FEBRUARY 10TH

Remembered especially my United Methodist brothers in prayer. We need one another. Trusting in the Holy Spirit.

We worshipped at Riverside UMC in Muncie. It was a lengthy service with much lay participation. Friends greeted us.

We enjoyed ourselves at the Olive Garden. So grateful I have the financial resources to do these things.

Re-read a letter some years ago from Bob DeLong. He was my district superintendent while at Seymour First UMC. He recommended me for the cabinet, but I was turned down.

Walked in Muncie Mall and had a long period of pondering and reflecting. I need more faith, O Lord, for the victorious living of these days.

MONDAY, FEBRUARY 11TH

Precious memories, how they linger; how they ever flood my soul. Sometimes in prayer it is inspirational to remember back more than sixty years ago.

Went to annual meeting of the Indiana Partners for Christian Unity and Mission at Saint Joseph Mother House in Tipton, Indiana. I wore three hats: chair of the Christian Unity Committee (North Indiana UMC Conference); representative of UMC Conference Council Director; and representative of Indiana UMC Bishop Michael Coyner. Visited with old friend Robert Welsh, president of Council on Christian Unity for the Disciples of Christ. We first met in the 1970s. Also spent quality time with Len Jepson, who creatively mixes humor and seriousness. I preached his installation sermon at First English Lutheran Church in Mishawaka seven years ago.

East central Indiana is really my home. The counties of Henry, Delaware, Jay, Randolph, and Wayne predominate.

Showbiz mentality in religious presentations, radio or TV, has bothered me for many years. There is a crassness that tends to cancel the genuineness of the Gospel message.

We pastors never know who will find our calling cards or when they will be used to contact us for various services. Some of those happenings, such as funerals or weddings, for me have led to beautiful works of the Holy Spirit!

TUESDAY, FEBRUARY 12TH

Hail Mary, full of grace; the Lord is with you. Blessed are you among women. Blessed is the fruit of your womb, Jesus.

Yes, and, Holy Mary, Mother of God, pray for us sinners now and at the hour of our death. Never underestimate the power of this woman!

Spent much of the day bringing administrative detail up-to-date. There were letters to write and phone calls to make.

Set up two more book signings for March. One at Books-A-Million in Kokomo, Indiana and one at Family Christian Bookstore in Carmel, Indiana.

Watched primary returns much of the evening. This Obama fellow truly is a phenomenon! O Lord, grant Your will be done and Your ways prevail.

WEDNESDAY, FEBRUARY 13TH

During this time of pause in my life, more faith, dear Lord, more faith. Teach me to drink more deeply from Your eternal wellsprings.

Cal Thomas's column on conservatism in *The Star* was exceptionally well done. Too many Republicans have one foot stuck in the mud!

Rotary program and board meeting at New Castle were profitable. They are such good folks and I enjoy them.

Reflected on Terri Johns, Fort Wayne Roman Catholic representative to IPCUM, who was at the recent meeting. She is devout and committed.

Gave thanks for two top-of-the-line principals, where I taught school in the mid- and late-1950s. They were Darrel Finch at Redkey, Indiana and Thomas Thomas Jr. at Dunkirk, Indiana.

THURSDAY, FEBRUARY 14TH

Your grace, O God, Your grace! In mystery and yet in reality we receive Your Body and Your Blood, O Christ, Savior, and Lord!

Book signing now scheduled for Barnes and Noble in Bloomington, Indiana in March. Dates for the month almost filled. Grateful.

Thank You, O Lord, for who and what I am. Take me and spiritually form me in Your likeness and that of the apostles.

Went to Barnes and Noble in Carmel, Indiana to pick up royalty payment. Sometimes those things can be complicated and drawn out.

Dorothy and I ate at our favorite MCL in Castleton (Indianapolis). We had exchanged loving valentines prior to that.

FRIDAY, FEBRUARY 15TH

Thank You, Lord, for another precious day. Sometimes I like the comforts of this life too much! I ask for forgiveness.

Reflected on my first appointment as a resident pastor from June of 1959 to June of 1962. It was Philadelphia UMC near Greenfield, Indiana. In the early months, I would walk alone in and around the little white wooden-framed building with a sense of pride and responsibility. So grateful and excited! Among the caring and gracious people were Bob Arthur, Avery and Dorothy Leary, Ida Martin, Catherine Donley, Lelia Bateman, Pete Mann, Gene Copeland, Herman Cook, Rex and Marjorie Sears, Mabel Jacobi, and Hazel Ashcraft. My predecessor was a student pastor, so they were aware of some of my lack of experience and having more zeal than knowledge. However, having taught school prior to that appointment, I was likely more mature than some.

One of our many pleasant vacation experiences was eating ice cream in Ludington, Michigan (1989).

Continue to remember with great appreciation and fondness Waldo Adams of the Leesburg UMC. I relished our conversations. We were much alike. I have seldom sensed such complete rapport. He was a man for all seasons with not only facts at his fingertips, but wisdom.

Hanging tough but tender with the Holy Spirit changes circumstances and creates newness that calms and yet energizes people.

SATURDAY, FEBRUARY 16TH

Hear my prayers, O Lord. Act on them as You see fit. Your presence is always my primary need. Eventually, everything and everyone fall into Your appointed place.

Dorothy and I visited The Glass Museum in Dunkirk, Indiana. What a treat! The display was worth anyone's time. I remembered some of the donors because of having taught in the high school there.

Recalled with special thanks Ruben H. Gums of WKTU in New York City, who interviewed me several months ago. It was about thirty minutes in length and was sent into the NYC metro area.

While I was pastor of Meadowdale UMC in Indianapolis (early 1980s), the pulpit committee of First Congregational Church in Detroit came to converse with me. They treated my wife and me to a long evening of food and carefully planned conversation. Then they visited my church on Sunday morning to hear me preach. They were certainly interested, but the position was not offered. It appeared they were deadlocked on two of us and decided to move in another direction. It was one of those great, old historic churches that is now closed.

Christ is purifying His Bride, the Church, and many of us are a part of that purification.

SUNDAY, FEBRUARY 17TH

Privileged to worship again in a congregational setting. O Lord, our adult years show many of us have three thousand Sundays!

Dorothy and I went to New Burlington UMC, southeast of Muncie, to worship. We were met affectionately by some people we had known fifty years or more. I especially enjoyed friends Phil Lawson and Charles Kirklin. They are conscientious laymen and their wives are also an integral part of the church. As a young man, Grandfather Walradth was a member there. His older brother, Merrill, was a pillar in the church prior to World War II.

On this date in 1963, I performed the marriage of my brother Michael R. Lacy and Alecia Amburn. The ceremony was held in the Friends Church of Farmland, Indiana.

Early in my life I learned when God touches us for the ordained ministry, He does not let loose! Blessed submission is the only right way to respond.

Emotional highs can thrill us and we may need them, but beware we can become awfully big in our own eyes. Our greatness can be exaggerated.

MONDAY, FEBRUARY 18TH

Early morning worship with prayers, Scripture, and Holy Communion is the habit that has stabilized my life. Early in the morning our song shall rise to Thee!

Prepared my February newsletter for the Associates. Lack of donations causing a bit of a problem.

Much of the day was spent pondering and reflecting. One's childhood is very formative but sometimes so difficult to remember!

Three aunts were so good to keep in contact with me over the years. They were Marjorie (Lacy) Luellen, Erma (Lacy) Kleihauer, and Glendabell (Walradth) Mitchell. Each had her own unique contribution. Their handwriting in most cases was virtually impeccable.

Yes, many of our young people's lives are messed up today with drugs and casual sex. We can blame them openly and even vociferously, but that is not likely to help much. We can pour out our hearts in secret places to our Father and I am convinced that will help!

TUESDAY, FEBRUARY 19TH

Thank You, Lord, for caring for me and my loved ones. As I travel to and from Indianapolis, please grant a safe journey.

Arrived downtown at 7:00 AM and walked to the Indiana Roof Ballroom for the Annual Indiana Prayer Breakfast. Sat at the table of the current secretary of state of Indiana Todd Rokita. In fact, I sat beside him and we had an informal, friendly conversation. Bill Gaither was the main speaker and he shared his very successful life with us. Frankly, he is what he admitted: a better singer/song writer than speaker! I have now attended a dozen or so of these. This one seemed to provide more substance and inspiration than the others. Former secretary of the state of Indiana Ed Simcox has been the general chairman for some time and he does a remarkably fine job.

When some people keep complimenting you for your preaching and telling you what a great man you are, how do you respond? I simply point to the heavens and honestly remind them I am only a channel or instrument. Beware of the temptation to take credit and exaggerate your importance!

Even with our problems and heartaches, what a beautiful family God has given us. I am so grateful.

A sometimes insurmountable problem in our churches, regardless of denomination, is the lack of maturity found in staff/parish relations committees. Who evaluates the pastor? Hopefully, those who have both candor and kindness, plus a solid relationship with Jesus Christ.

WEDNESDAY, FEBRUARY 20TH

Early morning worship words were strong and distinct. Felt like I was doing a liturgy for a worship service or prelude to study.

Weather was inclement, so I headed for Rotary meeting in New Castle somewhat earlier than usual. Attendance down, but attitude and spirits good.

Spent the evening at the Phi Delta Kappa meeting in Ball State Alumni Center. Professor from Taylor University spoke on "Teaching the Holocaust

Content and Methodology." Reminded of the Jewish-Christian Resource Packet that Rabbi Jonathan Stein of the Indianapolis Hebrew Congregation and I put together close to twenty years ago. Midge Roof (Episcopalian), Jon Walters (UMC), and Monsignor Ray Bosler (Roman Catholic) were very helpful. More than four hundred packets were sold, mostly in the Midwest, and some seminars were held.

Sometimes, do laity attempt to bludgeon their pastors into submission with dollar bills? I confess that is not a nice inquiry! What is a positive response to such action? Pray without vindictiveness, my brothers and sisters.

Nearly all of the district superintendents to whom I reported missed opportunity after opportunity to lift up the imperative of Christian Unity. There is lingering sadness in that. Nevertheless, I give thanks to God for the vision He has imparted to me.

THURSDAY, FEBRUARY 21ST

Sing songs of praise to You, Redeemer and Lord! Call upon His name with thanksgiving day and night.

Breakfast with my brother, Mike, at the Sunshine Restaurant in Muncie. Delicious food and meaningful fellowship.

A truly memorable experience was going into the Ancient Accepted Scottish Rite in the Valley of Indianapolis. This happened in the Fall of 1971 in the Cathedral. I was pastor of Union Chapel UMC in the city at that time. Bill Bastian and Ed Arens were my sponsors. The Rose Croix degrees, in particular, were not only moving, but basically Christian and some of us shed tears with much emotion. Hugh Gunn (Tabernacle Presbyterian pastor in Indianapolis) was the orator and I was the chaplain. I return there from time to time to eat and visit the excellent library, where my books are available.

As we grow older, a life of prayer comes more naturally to some of us. We are in a position to be prayer warriors.

I earnestly hope and pray to leave a legacy to my children and grandchildren of being a genuinely good man. Of course, I trust the same is true for others, who have known me.

FRIDAY, FEBRUARY 22ND

Love is patient and kind. It is not jealous or boastful. It is not arrogant or rude. Capture our hearts, O Lord, and remold us!

How do you say thank you to all those who made contributions to your life? Remember special friends during undergraduate days at Ball State (1950–1954): Jon Rye Kinghorn and Dick Pugsley.

Really, there are no self-made men or women. We all are indebted to others, sometimes in ways hard to admit.

One of the greatest Christians I have ever known was Dr. A. Wesley Pugh. He was my district superintendent very early in my ministry. He was powerful in northern Indiana Methodism, but not so much so he wouldn't get on his knees and pray! Dr. Pugh treated me with loving firmness; I watched and listened very carefully. His model of ministry seems to have gone from us, but oh how we need it! He married Dorothy and me on November 6, 1959.

Death remains a mystery for all of us, but there are those assurances from above that tell us to have faith, hope, and love. Our heavenly Father is in charge and what else do we need to know?

SATURDAY, FEBRUARY 23RD

We must all get better acquainted with Jesus the Christ. He continually knocks at the doors of our hearts, hoping to gain entrance.

Went to Fishers where Dorothy, Donna, Sharon, and Martha went shopping for Sharon. It turned out to be mostly blissful frustration! While they were busy, I visited one of my long-time haunts, Half-Priced Books, near Castleton Square. Since retirement, I have bought far fewer books. Need to write more and read less.

Gave thanks for some professionals who have affirmed and written about my published writing and/or commitment to ecumenism. Hortense Myers of *United Press International* was a kind lady. Ruth Anne Lipka of *The Times-Union* (Warsaw, Indiana); Walter Skiba of *The Sunday Times* (Munster, Indiana); and Andre Salles of *The News* (Merrillville, Indiana) did features on my literary/ecumenical work.

In high school, I could count on both hands the dates I had. I had even fewer dates in college. My lack of money and timidity always seemed to show!

At one time or another, I suppose we all ask what each of us deserves. I have no answer to that, but I believe God does and that's fine with me.

SUNDAY, FEBRUARY 24TH

Lord Jesus, I love You with all my heart, soul, mind, and strength. Please send me more and more abundant living.

We worshipped at High Street UMC in Muncie. It was a quality service that was ordered, but not stuffy and stiff.

Spent much of the day preparing a lengthy paper on the president as pastor. Our next one must be pastoral. Just what all this implies, I do not know, but God does.

Praise God for the caring and stimulating social science professors I had at Ball State. They were very influential in forming my life from 1950 to 1954 and well beyond, even unto this very day. Special appreciation goes to Richard Caldemeyer, Everett Ferrill, Robert LaFollette, and Lawrence Scheidler. They were quite different men and gave me at the time a well-rounded view of the social sciences.

Praise God for everyone who has entered my life. Even when negative things occur, God's blessings are someplace to be found.

MONDAY, FEBRUARY 25TH

Just think—another day to give glory to God for Father, Son, and Holy Spirit! Seventy-five years translates into more than twenty-seven thousand days of giving thanks!

O God, I trust, hope, and pray most of my days have been pleasing in Your sight! You are always the final Judge.

Christian Unity Committee meeting in Kokomo. Excellent input from Jon Gosser and Chris Roberts. Lord, thank You for them.

How good it is to remember some of the greats in ecumenism. Grover Hartman, Dorothea Green, Harold Statler, and Bishop John D'Arcy come to mind.

Father, please forgive them who remain in their ghettos of denominational loyalty. We beg of You to lift more, many more, to the vision of Christian Unity.

TUESDAY, FEBRUARY 26TH

Great is Thy faithfulness, O God my Father. Fatherhood, with all of its failures, remains in place in the divine scheme of things.

Morning made up of telephone calls and promotional work. Always trust the Holy Spirit is abiding and providing.

About twenty-five years ago, the Holy Spirit spoke to me in no uncertain terms, indicating I would have a unique ecumenical ministry and a gift to give. I was at Meadowdale UMC in Indianapolis at the time. It is a fearful thing to fall into the hands of the Living God! I would have run away but couldn't move at the time. God had taken the initiative.

My brother and sister Roman Catholics have been both very helpful and inspirational. During my lifetime, Pope John Paul II has had no equal.

Noted my report cards during my third and fourth grades at Blountsville Elementary School (Indiana). Received mostly Bs, some As, and a few Cs. This was for the school year of 1941–1942. I was only in the third grade a few weeks and was then promoted to the fourth grade. Fifth and sixth grades were virtually straight As in the same school.

WEDNESDAY, FEBRUARY 27TH

Forgive us, O Lord, for our monstrous sins as a nation. We have continually and with persistence betrayed the highest and best we know.

Did book signing at Borders in downtown Indianapolis. The staff was very kind and considerate on a blistery day. Many interesting—even provocative—questions from those who came by my table to visit. Some of the best conversations are with those who do not buy books. The educational value from such experiences is immense!

Recalled with deep appreciation the chaplains for whom I worked briefly, as a chaplain's assistant, during my stint on active duty with the U.S. Navy (1955–1956). This occurred at the naval base in Newport, Rhode Island.

At my baccalaureate service, class of 1950 at Center High School, our speaker was Russell Ford. He was widely known for his appearances on the Cadle Tabernacle Broadcast from WLW in Cincinnati. C.H.S. was located in Perry Township of Delaware County in Indiana. It no longer exists.

At my commencement, same class and location, Ray Montgomery was the speaker. Charles O. Jordan was the valedictorian. My father, Charles William Lacy, gave both the invocation and benediction.

THURSDAY, FEBRUARY 28TH

Thanks be to God, Who sends us our Savior and Lord to heal our broken hearts and enable us to have abundant living.

Slower moving around today. I must be getting older, not old, mind you! O immortal God, stay close by.

How many close clergy friends does a clergyman have in this life? Perhaps fewer than most folks, for various reasons. I remember three, in particular: Harold Bachert, Jim Willyard, and Dan Motto. All were United Methodists. I would also include Ron Liechty (UCC), Monsignor Cornelius Sweeney (RC), and Father Thomas Murphy (RC).

Among UMC bishops, Ralph T. Alton was the most personable and respectful of my talents. Political realities seemed to keep him from being less than he could be!

Dear God, keep us as clergy ever so close to You and in doing so relating well to one another as brothers.

FRIDAY, FEBRUARY 29TH

Our God is One of powerful love and loving power. How truly magnificent He is! When I survey my past and present, I perceive the hand of God. I do not expect that to change in the future.

Called to do a committal service by New Burlington UMC for Charles Yeager at the Garden of Memories, north of Muncie. The service went well and enabled me to do public ministry for the first time in awhile.

I celebrate the numerous opportunities of being an ordained minister. I am grateful, deeply grateful, for these many years.

Thanks to Gloria Reed, Paul Robb, and Maggie Nixon of the Plymouth, Indiana *Pilot News*. Their published words over the years about me and my ministry were appreciated.

I note by the date today that it is a leap year. How fitting for doing a personal/professional memoir!

MARCH
2 0 0 8

SATURDAY, MARCH 1ST

Repentance, forgiveness, and restoration make up the spiritual trilogy of many of our lives. Leaving out one phase can thwart our abundant living.

Attended men's Lenten breakfast at New Burlington UMC. It was a well-handled event with pastors recognized and appreciated.

Did book signing at Walden's in Anderson. Thank You, Father, for all these events that continue to add to a varied and certainly worthwhile ministry.

Recall leadership academy experiences in Warsaw, Indiana (1987–1988) and Muncie (2002–2003). Both were excellent!

Some trouble in my spirit, but as the day moved to conclusion, I felt an uplifting and quieting of my being.

SUNDAY, MARCH 2ND

Thanksgiving and praise to our Creator, Who was before the beginning and after the ending of all things. Such greatness, O God, I cannot comprehend.

We worshipped in Muncie. Thank You, Lord, for the variety in worship Your churches provide us.

Went to Fishers on behalf of Sharon to help her with her apartment living. Took her and my wife to dinner in an upscale restaurant.

Enjoyed a time of relaxation and reading in Borders of Carmel, Indiana, where I had done a recent book signing.

Very tired and can't seem to recuperate. God has given me splendid health, but I must be careful of that which comes with aging.

MONDAY, MARCH 3RD

Holy God, purify us and reconcile us with one another, especially those who claim the Christian Faith. Then the world has reason to believe!

Remembered MDIV (BD) days at Christian Theological Seminary (late 1950s and early 1960s). Special friends were Paul Mitchell, Dale Wilson, Joe Kipfer, Art Vermillion, Arleon Kelley, and Ray Whitton. Each made a contribution to my life during those early days of preparation for the ordained ministry. Art and Ray were members of the Disciples of Christ. The others were Methodists. However, soon after graduation, Paul affiliated with the International Council of Community Churches and spent many years in New Jersey. Paul (or "Pete") was the best man at my wedding. I was best man at Dale's wedding. To the best of my knowledge, all have had significant ministries for which I am grateful and blessed. In those days, we all needed to mature and did!

We cannot fully know what is in other people's lives and that is why we must take the log out of our own eyes before we try to remove the speck out of theirs.

Often fascinated by the wisdom in the Book of Proverbs. In its own uniquely brilliant way it provides an encompassing philosophical statement for life.

So grateful for having lived in places like the Chicago area where one has access to so much in so many different ways. It's a long way from Blountsville, Indiana to a metropolitan area of six million people with diversity that is almost unimaginable!

TUESDAY, MARCH 4TH

The love of God, how rich, how pure! Grant that we, O God, might be pure. Melt and mold us to your specifications.

Rain, sleet, and snow came down on us. The driving became dangerous. I stayed home!

For many years, Roman Catholic priests have made their positive imprints on my life and ministry. This was especially true of Monsignor Cornelius Sweeney. When I was at Seymour First UMC (Indiana), he was at Saint Ambrose in the same city. We often shared our lives and ministries. "Cornie," as we called him, had been vicar general of the Archdiocese of Indianapolis. In 1977, we decided to lead the first Community Thanksgiving Service ever held at Saint Ambrose. The mayor spoke, the church was packed, and the choir from Seymour First UMC sang from the balcony!

Really, spiritual formation is what our lives are all about. The goal of our lifetime is to be formed in the likeness of Christ and the apostles.

I believe Mother Angelica is right. She says the hard problem is deciding what ministry to do and then the money will be there. Of course, from another viewpoint, we are to be in ministry during our every breathing moment.

WEDNESDAY, MARCH 5TH

O God, keep us ever humble before Your throne. Please supply our needs, recognized and unrecognized.

Serious driving problems in Muncie area. Ice two inches thick some places on the streets. Treacherous.

Awesomely surprised about three years ago at this time. Received call from a reporter in Louisville, representing *Time* magazine. He wanted to do an extended interview in regard to my views on the Blessed Virgin Mary. He indicated he understood I had been a long-time advocate of theologically placing her in a more prominent place in Protestantism. Of course, he was right. Soon after the interview, photographer Robert A. Davis from Chicago called and came to Muncie. He took pictures in both the Madison Street UMC (Muncie), where I was a retired supply pastor at the time, and in my home. So, I became a part of the magazine's cover story with both a brief interview and a picture in the March 21, 2005 issue!

Regretfully, two or three of my appointments were not long enough for parishioners to experience both my intellectual and pragmatic, yes, and my professional and personal sides. Affirmation of my ministry on the part of district superintendents in charge could have saved the day.

People invariably have axes to grind, in and out of the churches. Pastors are called to be nonjudgmental and listen as faithfully as they can without neglecting others under their care.

THURSDAY, MARCH 6TH

Abundant living, dear God, is our goal for this life and will help prepare us for eternity. Teach us that it comes as a gift and often with trial and travail.

Coffee with Ron Johnson at a local restaurant. I appreciate his Wesleyan and Missionary Church background.

A highlight of the various services clubs to which I have belonged over the years and across the state was being a member of Indianapolis Downtown Kiwanis. Two members of the Indianapolis Hebrew Congregation sponsored me: Rabbi Jon Stein and Robert Levin. The membership at the time I was there (1982–1985) read like a "Who's Who." Even Mayor Bill Hudnut was a member, along with Henry C. Ryder, Gene E. Sease, and Morris E. Thomas Jr. Special friendships were: Sol Blickman, James E. Bettis, Wade Rubick, Charles J. Somes, and J. Russell Townsend. Sol, James, Wade, Charles, and Russell all became members of my ecumenical network (Lacy and Associates).

We can often be weighted down with worldly values that only perpetuate the necessity of holding tightly to things and attitudes that really do not matter in the long run. Clergy can be just as engulfed in this as laity. We are called to higher and better values.

Our flesh and blood need the flesh and blood of our dear Savior and Lord, Jesus the Christ.

FRIDAY, MARCH 7TH

O Lord, thank You for enabling me to be born again by the blood of Your son, my Savior and Lord!

Snow storms are coming through just south and east of us. Cincinnati is experiencing a blizzard. Columbus, Ohio got twenty inches of snow!

Dorothy and I had lunch with Merrill and Joan (Pease) Felton. It was an enjoyable time of reminiscing and conversation.

We both feel the need for more socializing with people with whom we feel comfortable. My individualism sometimes gets in the way.

We also went out in the evening to eat at an old favorite, the Olive Garden. It was a pleasant and rewarding day.

SATURDAY, MARCH 8TH

Sometimes, O God, our hearts cry out for decidedly improved human relations! Indeed, Christians are never citizens of this world, but they try to make it better.

Trip to Family Christian Bookstore in Indianapolis (Cherry Tree Mall) for signing. It was a delightful surprise with many copies being sold.

Thankful for Jewish-Christian dialogues presented by Harriet L. Kaufman (Cincinnati). As a Jewish laywoman, her seminars have been quite helpful in many places and covering most of thirty years.

Always appreciated the Ecumenical Society of the Blessed Virgin Mary, based in England. It does so much internationally.

Precious Lord, grant I would always seek to be a genuinely good man, motivated to do what is right and refrain from doing wrong.

SUNDAY, MARCH 9TH

How good You are to me, O Lord! Day and night and night and day, Your presence abides. Please grant that I will always be a man of faith and practice.

Strange set of circumstances kept us from attending worship. I was sorry about that and trust God was forgiving.

We enjoyed eating out. I am so grateful to have the financial resources to do this. Dorothy is such a good partner.

Received phone call from Clyde D. Wake, who followed me at Princeton First UMC (now Hillside) in southeastern Indiana. He appreciated my intercessory prayer for him. Among the key laity in that church were Bill and Phyllis Hitch, C. Kightly Trippett, James McDonald Jr., Sally Hart, Mary Kolb, and Bob and Mame Bates.

Fear only Him who can send you to the grave and eternal punishment. That's solidly and biblically based preaching, but are there any listeners who will consider the validity of it?

MONDAY, MARCH 10TH

Sweet hour of prayer, sweet hour of prayer. What an unmatched privilege it is, O Lord, just to be in Your presence!

It was a day filled with preparing taxes that soon must be filed. Fortunately, the information is at hand.

I beg of You, Lord, not to allow me to be proud of the gifts I gave in 2007. Twenty percent of my income seems generous, but it really isn't!

Keep me ever humble so that my mostly hidden witness of stewardship remains a blessing to and for others.

Thank You, Lord, for my being and doing. My finances belong to You. I just want to make a significant contribution in harmony with the Holy Spirit.

TUESDAY, MARCH 11TH

Stay close by, Lord. I am nothing but a converted sinner saved by the grace of a merciful God! Thank You.

Reflected on my pastorate at First UMC Hagerstown, Indiana from 1966 to 1970. Overall, these were years of solid growth. Special people were Bob Pierce, Paul R. Foulke, Bud Gray, Jim and Martha Giggy, Eddie O'Neel, Ben Yeager, Vera Hoover, Arnold Doughtery, and Onie and Mary Cain. Paul was the postmaster, Bud was the funeral director, Eddie was the local newspaper editor, and Arnold was a county commissioner. Among the vibrant and forward-looking young couples were Bob and Carol Meyer, Ralph and Joan Lafuze, Dale and Karen Leonard, Don and Connie Hilbert, and Fred and Jayne Bennett. There were major challenges during those years that included the trauma of Dana Corporation buying Perfect Circle, my throat surgery, and the complete renovation of the sanctuary.

Praise God for His patience and mercy! Without them, how can we expect more than a death without hope?

My Salem UMC (1985–1987) appointment gave me a sense of the Liturgy of the Word and Liturgy of the Sacrament. It filled a deep need within me and I shall be forever grateful.

In joy or sorrow, success or failure, always thank the ever-living God for all opportunities.

WEDNESDAY, MARCH 12TH

Savior, like a shepherd lead us. I am one of Your sheep, sometimes bewildered and confused, but never lost.

Great Rotary meeting in New Castle with Judge Mike Peyton speaking! Nearly fifty people in attendance. Our board meeting followed and we conducted essential business. Beverly Hankenhoff, Wil Ruback, Paul Rhodes, Maurie Goodwin, Megan Luecke, and Mark Schoettmer were very helpful. What a joy it is to be among the New Castle Rotarians! As their president this year, they have given me excellent support. Kit Crane, Henry County prosecutor and incoming president, has worked carefully with me and I am indebted to his loyalty.

I have often thought over the years how alive and well the ecumenical spirit is in some service clubs. I am still not sure what that says about the churches!

While all pastors are spiritual directors, some of us have felt called to do this ministry well beyond our local churches.

Several laity I have sought to serve in different churches attempted to force secular values on me and, thereby, expected the parish to be led by such a style. One dear lady in Rushville Saint Paul UMC once said to me, "Forgive them, for they know not what they do!"

THURSDAY, MARCH 13TH

When the roll is called up yonder, I'll be there. Many of us grew up with those lyrics and sincerely hoped to be received into heaven.

Some, of course, who profess the Christian faith, say heaven or a blissful hereafter doesn't matter. They need to read the New Testament more carefully!

The meeting in Indianapolis of the Religion Communicators Council was positive. Dan Gangler of UMC Communications provides inspired leadership.

While the Holy Spirit is our guide, it takes expertise as well to enable us to do ministry. Hopefully, the Holy Spirit pervades all we do.

I am praying for our president and all who hold authority and responsibility for our nation. O God, are we really morally bankrupt?

FRIDAY, MARCH 14TH

Lord Jesus, thank You for Your loving protection. How often I have escaped automobile accidents and been reminded of Your powers!

Off to Books-A-Million in Kokomo for signing. Very appreciative of the staff's sensitivity. One lady bought four copies! Human interaction on these treks never ceases to amaze me. We seem to run the gamut of economic, social, political, and religious views. This bookstore is well-situated on Highway 31 between Indianapolis and South Bend.

Grateful for those at *The Vidette-Messenger* in Valparaiso (mostly in the 1980s) who wrote features about me and my ministry: Chuck Knebel, Rich Lowery, and Toni Griffith-Byers.

Thought of Frank Tolbert (attorney) in Logansport, Indiana. He is an Episcopalian layman with biblical and theological education that would top most of us. His contributions to the conservatives in the Anglican Communion is substantial.

Christian Unity ministry, totally separate and apart from interreligious dialogue, can be injurious to our best ecumenical purposes. Jews, Christians, and Muslims are all children of Abraham.

SATURDAY, MARCH 15TH

Praise God for the ongoing opportunities of this life! Hopefully, what we do here and now translates into eternal goodness.

Went to Gethsemane UMC here in Muncie to be guest speaker at a District United Methodist Men's Lenten breakfast. Great crowd! I spoke mostly on my literary ministry and how expansive it is. Read briefly from *Fast Food for the Soul* and *More Fast Food for the Soul*. There seemed to be excellent rapport with the audience of about one hundred or so. Several from Yorktown UMC were in attendance. Also managed to insert some serious ecumenism from time to time.

Did a book signing at Family Christian Bookstore in Carmel. Sales about average. Conversations very rewarding.

I find happiness and contentment in the Holy Trinity. Jesus is my Savior and Lord; I am seeking to do the will of the Father and the Holy Spirit is my guide.

Thank God, He shows us sometimes how little and insignificant we are without Him.

SUNDAY, MARCH 16TH

O God, Protector and Guide, grant us Your holiness as an ideal for all. Lift us to those higher heights.

Off to Barnes and Noble in Bloomington, Indiana to do a book signing. They knew I would be early, so they were waiting on me. Good signing! Sold more copies of my *Collected Works* than usual. Kevin Giggy bought a copy. Kevin's father, Jim, and mother, Martha, were close to us in our Hagerstown pastorate. When I went there in 1966, his father was chair of the Pastor/Parish Committee.

Gave thanks for God's protection. The trip was accident-free and people along the way were considerate. Southern Indiana has some precarious roadways!

If I could live to be hundreds of years old, I believe there would be ministry to do and I would find satisfaction in it!

We must not apologize for being of the male gender. It is a magnificent and holy honor. The only way it can be taken from us is if we give it away and, indeed, some men are doing that very thing!

MONDAY, MARCH 17TH

Please be ever near us, Lord, especially Dorothy. Even with her health problems, she has gallantly fought the good fight.

Spent the morning doing correspondence. I am seventy-five years old and it seems there is so much yet to be done!

Reflected on my pastorate at Saint Paul UMC in Rushville, Indiana. It was a brief stay and with poor district administration. Strange as it may sound, our four beautiful teenage daughters created more than a little jealousy. This became a factor in our moving. That there were key people in the church who saw it as little more than another social organization was also a negative factor. Five elderly women rallied behind our family: Mary Louise Wilson, Adelaide Von Ohlen, Phil Schermer, Grace Alexander, and Eulia Sedam. Upon leaving, we were presented with a sizeable gift.

Truly, good and right deeds flow from a person spiritually formed by the Holy Spirit. Faith and works meet in harmony.

Am I a contemplative pastor? Well, that is a strong aspect of my personality and perhaps growing stronger.

TUESDAY, MARCH 18TH

O God, continue to teach me that the long view of life (and death) is truly what counts. Be patient with me, Lord Jesus.

My column for *The Star Press* (Muncie) is to appear on Holy Saturday. Asked Holy Spirit to provide thoughts and words.

Grateful to have correspondence with William Murchison of *The Dallas Morning News* from time to time. He is a conservative Episcopalian.

Reminisced about the brilliant lectures presented by Walter Sikes at Christian Theological Seminary during my MDIV work (1958–1961). What a giant!

For two years (1962–1964) at Trinity UMC in Kokomo, Pete and Ruth Puterbaugh were like parents to me. Should have stayed longer!

WEDNESDAY, MARCH 19TH

Praise be to You, O God, for Your watchful care and countless mercies. I love Your Kingdom, Lord.

Early speaking engagement with the New Castle Breakfast Optimist Club. Splendid bunch of folks! In my presentation, I pointed out many of my relatives, including my father, mother, and grandparents, who were laid to rest in Blountsville and Mooreland cemeteries. My remarks were well received, especially the readings from *Fast Food for the Soul*. Several glad to purchase copies.

Noon New Castle Rotary gathering was positive and enjoyable, as usual. Believe my pastoral ways are an asset to them.

Why is depression almost always considered a negative experience? I have found it to be a healing time, which makes us more dependent on God.

I tend to shy away from those who insist on being born again, mostly because their interpretation of this event is so rigidly defined.

THURSDAY, MARCH 20TH

Thank You, Lord, for Your loving care. Indeed, Who else can care for us in any serious and unlimited way?

Mostly correspondence and the writing of checks during the morning hours. Sent a special gift to First Friends Church in New Castle, honoring Gene Lacy.

O God, help us to affirm and give thanks for those many who volunteer hours of time and loads of talent!

Service to and for others keeps human relations moving in positive directions. Rotary has it right: service above self.

For those millions who received Holy Communion this day, I give humble thanks. Ah, the Body and Blood of our Blessed Savior and Lord!

FRIDAY, MARCH 21ST

You are my Redeemer, Lord Jesus, and my destiny is in Your hands. As some would say, I have put all my eggs in one basket!

Yes, precious Jesus, there is stability, security, and even serenity in our relationship. I seek no other.

Attended the Good Friday Service at First Presbyterian Church in Muncie. It was a marvelous performance, but not sure how worshipful for most people that were present. Helpful visit during the service with Bob Burton, former chaplain of Ball Hospital here in Muncie. Bob is a solid fellow (American Baptist).

My wife and I went to Texas Roadhouse in Anderson for dinner. We had our usual pleasant time of sharing. I love her so much.

It is important to give credit to the United Methodist Church for some of its ecumenically oriented programs and formats, especially through the Upper Room.

SATURDAY, MARCH 22ND

Soon-to-be-risen Christ, the heavens quake and humanity is in awe. A mystery and yet profound reality is given birth.

It was a day of travel to and from Mishawaka/South Bend for another signing in a Family Christian Bookstore. It was refreshing to converse with Catholics there. The chain of stores is known for its conservative Protestant materials. The Holy Spirit is much at work in such businesses and relationships. This is very encouraging and I am delightfully inspired by such happenings!

In the Scottish Rite Cathedral (South Bend) in 1996, I presented "A Letter to a Roman Catholic" at a joint Knights of Columbus/Scottish Rite breakfast. The fellows decided if they could play golf together, they could do a Lenten series together with both Protestants and Catholics speaking! Copies of that presentation have been widely distributed.

How magnificent and hope-giving it was to provide worship on Lake Tippecanoe (1987–1990) in the heat of the summer!

As I grow older, I am continually amazed—even startled—by the seemingly endless number of independent, nondenominational ministries.

SUNDAY, MARCH 23RD

Christ has risen! We serve a risen Savior and Lord. He is not a dead Jewish prophet, still lying in the grave.

Dorothy and I worshipped at Fishers UMC. It was a uniquely inspirational service that brought tears to my eyes.

Then, we picked up our daughter Sharon and took her with us to The Hawthorns Country Club in Fishers. Daughter Donna and son-in-law Terry are members there. We were all treated to delicious food at their expense! It was so good to have all of our family together again for a time of fulfilling sharing. It is one of those splendid events each year that we have grown to expect, and with gratitude.

The whole day was marked by happiness and contentment. I am very proud of my children and grandchildren. We are so blessed!

Recall with deep appreciation a letter from an Aunt (Lacy) thanking me for giving money so my grandparents could have a tombstone. Grandmother Lacy did not want to be placed in an unmarked grave. Bless her heart!

MONDAY, MARCH 24TH

Give us the Easter glow, O Lord, so we can share it with others. They, too, hunger and thirst for abundant living.

We Christians are so privileged, whether we have joys or sorrows. Our great mistake comes in believing we must always succeed in a secular sense.

Our nation is moving through uncharted waters. We really need You, Lord. Our strength and wisdom alone are so inadequate.

Went to Marion, Indiana to have our taxes figured. This always seems to be a grueling session, but it is necessary!

I cherish the life You have given me, Lord, and trust my stewardship of it is acceptable to You.

TUESDAY, MARCH 25TH

My life and my all, I owe to You, Lord, my Redeemer. All of creation is Yours and shall always be.

Went to Liberty-Perry Township School Corporation here in Delaware County, Indiana. Very revealing old records. Discovered my grades for the time I was a student well over fifty years ago at Center High School. Better than I remembered! Apparently, I finished third in a graduating class of sixteen with about a ninety percent average. History was easily my strongest subject. When I was in grade school in Blountsville, Indiana, that was also the case. In fact, that carried throughout college and seminary. American history, in particular, was my forte. I loved all periods. Perhaps the Colonial period was my favorite.

Attended annual banquet of the New Castle-Henry County Chamber of Commerce. It was held at the spacious First Baptist Church.

Advice to those new to the ministry: don't stay in the membership rolls, the church building, or the parsonage!

Wesley's *Covenant Service* is a true gem. I have used it many times and always found it inspirational.

WEDNESDAY, MARCH 26TH

Do not judge others and God will not judge you. Do not condemn others and God will not condemn you. Forgive others and God will forgive you.

In long-studied reflection, I believe some of my sour relationships in particular churches were experienced at the point of my being bent toward introversion. Most United Methodist people seem to relate better to extroverted pastors. Well, friends, I can only be who and what I am! Come to think of it, a professional counselor once told me I would be more comfortable in the Lutheran Church.

Rotary meeting was a blessing. Joy filled the air, especially celebration of New Castle-Henry County citizens of the year. Awards were given to Carol Goodwin and Dick Leitch.

Paused, thankfully, to think about my ecumenical Associates over the years. Many have shared my vision and commitment. In a way, they have become my disciples.

Fort Wayne's *Journal Gazette* provided features about my ministry twenty or so years ago. Gabriella Jacobs did a feature on my literary/ecumenical ministry lifting up the Blessed Virgin Mary. Lori Nims did a three-page Sunday education feature on the lake ministry I developed on Tippecanoe Lake. Lori's piece was remarkable for the space utilized and the pictures presented. My thanks to them! These were published during my appointment to the Leesburg UMC (1987–1990).

THURSDAY, MARCH 27TH

O precious host of witnesses, who now resides in heaven with our Savior, thank you for your ongoing prayers of intercession.

Spent the morning on ecumenical ministry. I give humble thanks for this calling that never seems to diminish.

Remembered with deep appreciation my appointment to Kokomo Trinity UMC from 1962 to 1964. What a change from my prior appointment! My new church was an impressive, newly renovated building near Delco Radio. The sanctuary was very attractive and colorful in the best sense of the word. The educational wing was less than ten years old. The factories in the area were very busy and the employees numerous. I worked hard and we added to both membership and attendance. Key laity were: Pete and Ruth Puterbaugh, Keith Baker, Bobbi Downhour, Martha McGowan, Katherine Harris, Walt Pring, Don Correll, Norma Taber, Tom Crowder, and Jim Thomas.

Twenty or so years ago, a Lutheran friend of mine told me that it is not possible to do both a pastoral and prophetic ministry at the same time. As hard as it is for me to admit, there is truth to this.

We must all learn sooner or later that loved ones in our families first of all belong to God and then to us.

FRIDAY, MARCH 28TH

Lord, I love You with all my being. Please forgive all of my sins of commission and omission.

Dorothy and I spent the morning in Fishers sitting with our new grandson, Justin Daniel Graham. What a joy he is!

Deeply concerned about the United States of America. My love for this nation and background in teaching American history have come to the forefront. O God, I beg of You, please forgive our countless sins! As a nation, collectively and individually, we have walked many wrong roads and continue to do so. Some do so brazenly, virtually spitting in the face of God! If need be, O Lord, painfully drive us to our knees!

Recalled one of the features I had written for *The South Bend Tribune* on the Founding Fathers. It dealt with their religious faith and continues to be apropos. Several people at that paper have been helpful to me, such as James Wensits, Paul Lamirand, Gene Stowe, Martha Rasche, and Howard Dukes.

To attempt to *use* the Holy Spirit may be the worst thing any of us can do. If we do so knowingly, dear God, we beg of You to forgive us!

SATURDAY, MARCH 29TH

Your providence, O God, is so far reaching we catch only a glimpse of it. You are mindful of humanity. Praise Your holy name!

Went to Terre Haute for a book signing at Books-A-Million. Mike, the store manager, was not only congenial, he was kind and supportive. Above average signing with many customers coming from east central Illinois. *Collected Works* continues to do well. Holy Spirit is surprising me!

I have enjoyed and felt privileged to preach Week of Prayer for Christian Unity sermons at both Saint Lawrence and Saint Mary Catholic churches here in Muncie. The rapport has been excellent and, I dare say, better than in some Protestant churches in which I have preached!

To live the Christian life seriously and with joy is to do so prayerfully. Everyday is a day of prayer. Pray wherever you are and whatever time it is!

How many miles have I driven in the cause of ministry for Christ and His Church? Certainly well over a million for starters.

SUNDAY, MARCH 30TH

Jesus Christ, Savior and Lord, You are my protector and guide. You miss nothing and in my dependence I am most grateful.

Worshipped at Methodist Temple UMC in Evansville. Vibrant service with jazz music that was exciting and appealing.

Did book signing at Borders. Kevin, store manager, excellent promoter of my books! He had sold copies before I arrived.

My initial feature on *Gems from James* was done in 1974 by George Stuteville of *The Evansville Courier*. Roger McBain of the paper has also been helpful.

Trip home, safe and sound, but tiresome. Heavy rains in southern Indiana. Arrived home about 1:15 AM.

MONDAY, MARCH 31ST

Lord God Almighty, keep our nation safe! Guide us into more fruitful pathways. Fill us with Your compassion.

Arose later than usual and took my time adjusting to the day. It felt good to relax and ponder the future. Dear Lord, You have provided so many wonderful opportunities.

During my time at Argos UMC (Indiana), I related to two really dedicated pastors there: Earl Lightfoot (Bible Church) and Jim Carter (Wesleyan Church). They were splendid colleagues.

During my active duty tour in the U.S. Navy, only one friend seems to come to the surface that I vividly remember; he was a pharmacist from Massachusetts named Edward L. Poznysc.

Recall with special gratitude Theresa Campbell and Keri S. McGrath of *Anderson, Indiana Herald-Tribune*. They wrote features on my ministry, especially the literary segment. John P. Cleary of the same paper took the picture that appears on the cover of my *Collected Works*.

APRIL
2 0 0 8

TUESDAY, APRIL 1ST

Slow me down, Lord, and quiet my heart and mind that I can—without question—sense Your presence.

It was mostly a day of planning, in detail, the month. So many good things for which I am grateful.

Recalled the bravery of my brother Joseph Allen Lacy during his two tours of duty as a helicopter pilot in Vietnam. Neither my brother Mike nor I could have done this for our country. He deserves a thank you that is permanent and should be passed on to the next generations. There have been so many good—even great—men in our military forces. Their sacrifices really are beyond my understanding, but not my gratitude.

Dear Lord, keep the American people safe and sound, but keep us also humble enough to repent of our sins.

What does Holy Communion do for the believer? For a starter, it reconciles, heals, cleanses, blesses, purges, and sanctifies.

WEDNESDAY, APRIL 2ND

O Thou long-expected Savior, come and dwell in our hearts and minds. We beg of You to do for us what we cannot do for ourselves.

UMC retired ministers breakfast was enjoyable and affirming. Widows of pastors are faithful about attending and are a positive addition, especially Hope Barnes.

Rotary meeting in New Castle both informational and inspirational. IPCUM part-time executive skillfully presented the ecumenical landscape in Indiana. We have been without a full-time executive for several years.

Grateful that I was able some years ago to support Joseph Thekkinen in India during his studies for the RC priesthood. He wrote to me several times in gratitude for my assistance financially and prayerfully. Joseph should now have been a priest for about twenty years.

Is the mosque replacing the church in England? There are signs that would indicate as much.

THURSDAY, APRIL 3RD

O Lord Jesus, You gave Your body and blood for me; yes, and You continue to do so! Even though at times I can be arrogant, selfish, belligerent, and hateful, You still love me!

Mostly a day of telephone calls, relaxing, and pondering. O dear God, restrain me that I will not try to get ahead of You.

Remembering my life throughout the teen years and how little of this world's goods we had. Our home was humble and probably close to the poverty level, even for that day and time. My father was ill and unable to work for months. We had no income of any kind. Finally, he became able to work for three dollars a day. These days lingered into my college days at Ball State. Promised my mother I would quit college and go to work full-time, but it never came to that.

My observation, generally, is too many Protestants sit in their pews visiting, thinking somehow they are honoring God as equals. Lacking is the sense of the awesomeness and infinity of His presence.

O Lord, help me not to abandon or disown or discount my achievements. The evil one would have me believe my life is over and mostly a failure. Well, that is God's business and I am the winner!

FRIDAY, APRIL 4TH

Always I thank my God! Indeed, Saint Paul knew what he was talking about. We must accept and imitate his insight.

Off to do a book signing at Family Christian Book Store in Plainfield, Indiana. Wow, is that area being developed! Surprisingly good signing. Traffic modest, but sales quite good. Very considerate customers. Gave thanks to God.

Recalled the prayer of Phillips Brooks, which begins, "Oh, do not pray for easy lives, pray to be stronger men . . ." For more years than I can remember, that prayer has been very helpful. I have sought to share it with countless numbers.

Arrived home before 11:00 PM and that was better than I expected. Happy to see my wife had waited up for me.

Is the time come for you to give thanks, integrate, and focus? At different times in our life, we are called to do exactly that.

SATURDAY, APRIL 5TH

Continue to teach me Your ways, O Lord, especially the virtue of loving patience. Remind me of Christ's sacrificial spirit.

Off to Walden's in Tippecanoe Mall in Lafayette. Store manager very cooperative and had done excellent promotional work. On the downside, several customers were rude and rejecting!

Pleasantly recalled what may have been my singular success at Ball State: excelling in my major, which was social science. During 1953–1954 was president of the Social Science Club. I also qualified for and joined the honor fraternity for that field, Pi Gamma Mu.

Eventually arrived home from that long drive to Lafayette with some frustration from the signing. Nevertheless, gave thanks to God for another opportunity.

O Lord, that we might touch the wellspring of the Eucharistic power of the ancient church.

SUNDAY, APRIL 6TH

All hail the power of Jesus' name, let angels prostrate fall! The God/Man is closer than our very skin.

After my wife and I worshipped, we went to Ruby Tuesday's for a luscious meal of steak and the trimmings. Grateful for such a lifestyle.

Wrote tax checks, along with checking the paperwork Bob Logan did for us. Seems we all need tax experts these days.

So pleased and inspired to peruse an autographed copy of *What Christians Should Know about Jews and Judaism* by Rabbi Yechiel Eckstein. He had signed it for me on Christmas Eve of 1984.

Despite trials, frustrations, temptations, and sometimes depressions, our Blessed Lord is always faithful.

MONDAY, APRIL 7TH

Holy Spirit of God, every morning we commune. Often I pour out my heart to You, sometimes in joy and sometimes in sadness. I sense that You are always listening.

Christian Unity meeting went well in Kokomo. Jon Gosser (Hobart, Indiana) and John Smith (Fort Wayne), who are UMC pastors, are dedicated ecumenists.

Some days I really miss our oldest daughter, Anne Marie. She died a tragic death in Chicago at the age of thirty-five. Her funeral was in Saint Athanasius Catholic Church in Evanston, Illinois. She rests in the love of God in Catholic Calvary Cemetery on the shore of Lake Michigan. So, until we meet again, dearest Anne, your father tries to keep the Faith and be loyal to the highest and best he knows.

My experience with Gideons is that they are fine, Christian individuals, who do their ministries faithfully. I have had them speak in most of my churches.

Have the male/female relationships in our society really degenerated? I believe so and they are continuing to do so, but never underestimate the grace of our God. The situation is not hopeless!

TUESDAY, APRIL 8TH

Hold me tightly, Lord, that I might not veer to the left or right. Keep me on the straight and narrow.

Produced promotional material for our conference-wide Christian Unity rally on Sunday, April 27th. Also made special mailing to area churches and key people.

Did some chores around the house. When couples get older, it is always better to share those necessities.

Spoke at New Castle Kiwanis club. Average age of group probably seventy-five! Good attention on the part of those present.

Gave thanks for my wonderful little family. As the years roll by, they mean more and more to me.

WEDNESDAY, APRIL 9TH

Lord of the Church, we beg of You to keep pulling us together that we may make a united witness to the world.

Excellent crowd at Rotary meeting! Great spirit with sharing of our joy of being together in service and fellowship.

So much to reflect upon during this year! God has been and is so good to me. He has protected and guided me all of my life. I am confident this is true of many others, but I can only speak for myself.

Gave thanks for those human beings who gave me the benefit of the doubt in questionable and controversial situations. They were helpful in enabling me to continue in my pastoral ministry.

Perhaps different from most, my very being and ministry have been interlocked virtually all of my adult years. My ministry with its many facets was never just a job or even a profession. It was always far more.

THURSDAY, APRIL 10TH

Call down Your Holy Spirit, Lord, and make it pervade all of our lives. Heal us and make us whole!

Mostly a morning of correspondence with letters of gratitude to others sent by God to enrich my life.

Learned Aunt Patty (Lacy) Keesling was having severe health problems. She is a good-hearted, hard-working person who means well.

Went to Danville, Indiana to the public library to make a presentation. In spite of excellent promotion, the crowd was sparse. Felt sorry for the young woman in charge.

Lacy and Associates, which became Lacy Institute for Ecumenism (LIFE), remains mostly a pride and joy. It has ecumenical influence.

FRIDAY, APRIL 11TH

Lord Jesus, come with Your healing compassion and soothe my soul. Only Your powers are adequate.

Ran errands and pulled loose ends together. So much to do before I leave for Chicago on Monday. Am I overextended? Well, it seems like I have been much of my life!

Spent an enjoyable and rewarding evening at Christian Theological Seminary. It was a special time for alumni to come together. Met Art Vermillion, Ed Filbey, and Charles Webb Jr. Art and I were in the seminary at the same time. Ed was on the counseling staff of Methodist Hospital in Indianapolis for many years. Charles works with the alumni association and gifts, including scholarships. While CTS has taken a liberal turn the last several years, I still enjoy and support its endeavors.

Returned home and had to confront some administrative detail with a bookstore. Does the left hand know what the right hand is doing?

During my pastorate at Leesburg UMC (1987–1990), I had feelers from a congregational church in Arizona. On the surface, it looked like a good match, but I was glad the negotiations broke down.

SATURDAY, APRIL 12TH

O God of love, justice, and mercy, enable me to be more dependent on You, remembering when I am weak I am strong!

Went to Fort Wayne to do book signing at Mitchells, a lovely and inviting store. Slow but consistent flow of people. Strong interest in my *Collected Works*.

Episcopalian bishops came to mind, who had added immensely to my ecumenical experiences. They were class in the best sense of the word. They were: William C. R. Sheridan (Northern Indiana), Edward W. Jones (Indianapolis), and William H. Brady (Fond du Lac, Wisconsin). All are now deceased. Bishop Brady was a part of my ecumenical network at one time. Bishop Sheridan was a magnificent cleric with all the bells and whistles, who could read from a telephone book and make you want him to continue! Bishop Jones and I spent much time together because of attending some of the same meetings together in Indianapolis over a period of years.

I have learned, sometimes painfully, that progress in my frame of reference does not jibe with God's will.

It is such a blessing to be forgiven for past failures in human relations and to know all is well!

SUNDAY, APRIL 13TH

Praises be to Jesus Christ, my Savior and Lord. My entire being is tied to this perfect Jewish fellow!

Worshipped at High Street UMC in Muncie. Jack Hartman's preaching was powerful and his theology was excellent.

Believe the most complete UMC pastor I have known is Richard E. Hamilton, long-time pastor of North Church UMC in Indianapolis. His practice of ministry positively covered all areas.

Prepared to depart tomorrow for Chicago and the National Workshop on Christian Unity. Over the years, I have already been a participate at twenty or so, almost always representing a group(s).

Dreading the drive up the interstates in Chicago, but look forward to seeing old friends, mostly committed ecumenists.

MONDAY, APRIL 14TH

This is my story; this is my song, praising my Savior all the day long. So, it should be for all who profess His name!

Left for the Marriott Inn in Chicago to participate in the National Workshop on Christian Unity. More fatigued than I realized and almost had a serious accident south of Merrillville, Indiana. However, arrived safe and sound. Accommodations were far more than adequate!

Opening worship service was at Mary Seat of Wisdom Catholic Church in Park Ridge. Dynamic music and inspirational leadership. Renewal of baptism vows during the service was especially uplifting. Clergy leaders walked among us and sprinkled us with water.

I have not walked by faith easily, but in my later years I have done much better. For that, I praise God!

It is so much better to let God set the agenda for our lives and the churches. It is a welcome relief to our self-centeredness.

TUESDAY, APRIL 15TH

More colossal opportunities, O God, among those who care about Christ's Holy Church! Thank you.

Informal breakfast provided by National Council of Churches. Observed many conversations that appeared positive for our ministry. Able to greet old friends, who have also attended this workshop across the years.

Michael Kinnamon (Disciples of Christ), new general secretary of the National Council of Churches, was the keynoter. His presentation was brilliant! He emphasized the life/work and faith/order dimensions must be held together in fundamental tension. My ministry in this field has usually come down on the side of faith/order. I have known Michael for most of thirty years and continually found him to be one of the brightest lights in the ecumenical movement.

Purify Your Church, O Christ, that she may be vibrant and holy. We give thanks for what we can be!

Certainly one of the most influential persons in my life was Monsignor Cornelius Sweeney. I think of him often and give humble thanks for his ministry to me at Seymour First UMC (1974–1979) and well beyond those years, even to this day.

WEDNESDAY, APRIL 16TH

Unity rings in our ears, O Christ! Please grant that it penetrate our hearts, minds, and very souls.

Reflected on last night's service at Saint Mary's Episcopal Church in Park Ridge. It was a joint service of Evangelical Lutherans, United Methodists, and Episcopalians. All members of these three denominations should have such an experience! There was joy and a sense of holy sharing.

Dirk Ficca, executive director of the Parliament of Religions, expanded our horizons beyond Christianity. It was profoundly helpful.

Evening worship at Baptist Congregational Church on the near south side of Chicago was powerfully moving! Two dear African American ladies gave me big hugs.

The promise of eternal life. It is a life beyond monetary purchase that is bought by the blood of our Savior and Lord. Hallelujah!

THURSDAY, APRIL 17TH

Dear Lord, I am getting older, but I can tell You are not finished with me yet in this life. So be it.

Closing session with luncheon at the workshop provided a panel of four, who challenged us. They were past-, present-, and future-oriented professionals. They were impressive, individually and collectively. It was a time of joyous goodbyes. Believe the consensus was we finished on a high note, refreshed, and ready to work even harder.

Trip home was smooth and quick for which I gave thanks. It felt good to be home and begin to catch up on other matters.

So thankful I never had to step out of the regular appointment process for those many years as a resident pastor (1959–2003).

While I never was directly involved most of the time in Sunday morning church school, I gave thanks for those laity who were willing to give their time, energy, and talent.

FRIDAY, APRIL 18TH

Faithfulness, above all else, You have taught me, O God! Grant all I am and do meets with Your complete approval.

The morning was one of playing catch-up. Very tired from my Chicago trip. Yet, recognizing in my depths God's will is being done in my life. In a way, we were all born to do His will and as we relate to others, we are called to respect that.

Took Dorothy to dinner at Texas Roadhouse in Anderson. The meals were plentiful and we did some meaningful sharing. Thank You, Lord, for this time.

Love divine, all love excelling! Precious Jesus, grant my life a safe journey throughout the night. There is so much more to be done.

From time to time, fasting has been a part of my self-discipline. I have usually taken Fridays for that, waiting until Saturday morning to eat again.

SATURDAY, APRIL 19TH

Love lifted me, love lifted me. When nothing else would help, love lifted me. Learned that as a little boy before I started to school.

Motored to Barnes and Noble (Glenbrook) in Fort Wayne for book signing. Two other authors were there sharing the time. Greeted, among others, by three UMC pastors: Ron VerLee of Fort Wayne, Mike Hendrix of Beech Grove (Indiana) and Bob Priest of Columbia City (Indiana). Other conversations were also rewarding.

Remembered and gave thanks for J. Richard Peck, a national communications director and editor for the UMC. This was especially true at the time he edited the *International Christian Digest* in the late 1980s.

Thankful I was at home at an early hour. Dorothy was not at all feeling good. She is a courageous woman.

I have pondered often how close we can be to a major spiritual breakthrough and then it doesn't happen! I am consoled by the fact that God understands this.

SUNDAY, APRIL 20TH

Holy Mary, Mother of God, pray for us sinners now and at the hour of our death. We must not forget the Blessed Virgin Mary!

We worshipped at Saint Andrew Presbyterian. Much of the service involved children and was delightful.

Then my wife and I enjoyed an appetizing meal at Ruby Tuesday's. It may have become Muncie's best overall restaurant.

Barry Wampler, former parishioner of mine at Argos UMC (Indiana) from 1991 to 1993, continues to be a valued friend and comrade. I am so pleased he has grown in the Faith through various channels, including hospital chaplaincy. I greatly value his judgment. He and his wife, Portia, have a lovely, large family.

Worked on some follow-up from the workshop in Chicago. I always do this and, as a result, have continued relationships with several wonderful people over the years. I only wish the other 99 percent of Indiana UMC could experience such events.

MONDAY, APRIL 21ST

He walks with me and talks with me; He tells me I am His own. What can be any better than that?

Produced monthly newsletter for my ecumenical colleagues. It was mostly about the NWCU I just attended.

Ran necessary errands to Staples and the post office. It takes a great deal to keep my retirement ministry going!

Remembered my years (1964–1966) as an associate pastor at College Avenue UMC in Muncie. Worked first under Don Barnes and then Curg Starkey. I was the bridge man in that often-difficult transition.

Laypersons who helped me to mature there were: Ralph and Betty Bushey, Dorothy Marshall, Joan Tharp, Ed Legg, Cree Gable, Fred McKinley, Eva Covalt, Meredith Church, Bill Locke, and Sally Rudicel.

TUESDAY, APRIL 22ND

Call upon the Lord for all your needs, known and unknown. He will answer your prayers in His way and His time.

Went to Rotary Club in Marion, Indiana to be their guest speaker. Alan Miller of Indiana Wesleyan University had invited me. I did my customary literary/ecumenical/pastoral approach. I cited Todd Rokita's grateful response to one of my little published stories about fathers and sons. He is the secretary of state of Indiana. Lo and behold, before I left, Todd came by without our knowing the other was there. It was a mysterious Holy Spirit moment!

Recalled with gratitude Bill Trimble, *The Rushville Republican* (Indiana) newspaper editor. During 1980–1981, he published my columns and the paper paid for them.

At times, I have felt like an alien in the United Methodist ministry. This can be traced—in particular—to my ecumenical orientation and individualism. Nevertheless, I give thanks!

The library at Grace College in Winona Lake, Indiana was a favorite place of mine during the Leesburg UMC (1987–1990) years. I did a great deal of research there.

WEDNESDAY, APRIL 23RD

Shout from the rooftops our Lord Jesus Christ has risen from the dead! Indeed, He has risen for you and me.

I need help from others, Lord, to sustain me in my faith. Please alert them to pray for me.

Rotary meeting in New Castle was free-flowing and pleasant. It was a gorgeous day with temperatures in the 70s.

Needed time to ponder and did so, alone and without obstructions. I have always been that way and have spent countless hours and sometimes days doing just that. It is frequently a means of both therapy and profound insights.

Learned old friend and UMC pastor Neal Partain had died in his sleep. He was also a former pastor of Seymour First UMC.

THURSDAY, APRIL 24TH

Give glory to God and affirm your faith, as your spiritual ancestors have done for centuries.

Mostly a day of ecumenical correspondence. Must continue to be led by the Holy Spirit in this ministry. Anything else would likely be fruitless in time and interfere with God's holy will.

Reflected on my prayers given everyday for colleagues and others for whom I sense a spiritual responsibility. The saints of the ages have taught us our prayer lives make or break us. To place the face of someone before you and lift up him/her before God is awesome intercessory ministry and we are most definitely called to do this very thing.

Breakfast with my brother Mike earlier in the day was enjoyable and satisfying. He is such a good brother!

One of the funniest/serious things I ever heard was of an evangelist saying nothing was happening in his friend's spiritual life, until he began to take out the garbage for his wife!

FRIDAY, APRIL 25TH

I give my burden to You, O Lord. Where else can I go but to the Lord? With Your presence and power all is well!

Went to a book signing at Books-A-Million on the northwest side of Indianapolis. Staff was marvelous. I enjoy the signings but sometimes the rejections, blatant and rude, are painful. Must be reminded this is God's business and to keep on doing what I am doing!

Recollected with powerful thanksgiving taking Holy Communion at two different times with Roman Catholics. The first was at Marian College in Fond du Lac, Wisconsin, where I was a keynote speaker for "Mary: Rediscovering the Meaning" in 1988. The second was at Saint Matthew Cathedral in South Bend with Bishop D'Arcy presiding.

Personal/professional ambition is so deceptive and, unless it is harnessed in harmony with the Holy Spirit, can be very hurtful and even disastrous.

When I saw commitment, maturity, and spiritual sensitivity in pre-marital counseling sessions, I was always so grateful.

SATURDAY, APRIL 26TH

Humble yourselves before God and in His own good time He will lift you up. I was a long time learning that and once in awhile backslide even yet!

Prepared newspaper column for *The Star Press* (Muncie). The benefits of the National Workshop on Christian Unity was the focus.

Did a book signing at Family Christian Book Store in Muncie. Visited with two of A. E. Helm's granddaughters. The Helm family is widely known for producing clergymen, especially for the United Methodist Church.

Relish knowing Edwin Johnson, UMC clergyman Wisconsin, who has been a key figure in my speaking in that state. I have appreciated his kindness and sensitivity.

Sensed more peace in my life. Believe it is coming from my obedience to the revelation given sometime ago.

SUNDAY, APRIL 27TH

O Lord, some days I try so hard and yet I am far from being perfect. Please help me to accept Your grace.

We worshipped at College Avenue UMC in Muncie. Except for a solo by an African American lady, the experience seemed wooden.

My wife and I ate our noon meal in a local restaurant and were disappointed in the service. Dear Lord, sometimes we grow spoiled!

Went to Christian Unity and Interreligious rally at Main Street UMC in Peru, Indiana. A small crowd, but very rewarding event. Representative from Islam was there.

So grateful I was able to spend many hours over the years with two UMC pastors, significantly younger than I am: Steve Kaehr and Scott Carmer.

MONDAY, APRIL 28TH

O God, only You can bring us peace that will pass all understanding. Help us to avoid forcing the issue on our own terms!

It was a busy day of correspondence. We are called to live in an attitude that continually praises God.

Reflected on the funerals of Great Aunt Pearl (McCall) Griffin, Aunt Arletta (Lacy) Jester, and Aunt Judith (Lacy) Harter. Had I not been appointed back to this part of the state, I would likely never have had the privilege of officiating at their services. Coming to Yorktown UMC, at the west edge of Muncie, as pastor opened up an old/new world of relationships. It has had a way of putting together the pieces of my life in ways that probably could not have been done in any other way. So, God's will is being done and His ways are prevailing.

I have always been inspired by church choirs singing the "Battle Hymn of the Republic." Trusting it will be sung at my funeral.

Convinced that had I not married Dorothy, I would never have married and may very well have been a priest (Anglican or Roman).

TUESDAY, APRIL 29TH

Count your blessings, name them one by one; see what the Lord has done. Friends, that's a good reminder!

As usual, did my early morning prayers with Holy Communion. Especially lifted up Aunt Patty (Lacy) Keesling and Uncle Bob Walradth. Both have heavy burdens of different sorts and I really care about them.

Worked on schedule for month of May. A printed schedule helps to keep my family aware of where I am and how to contact me.

Watched on television the ongoing debate involving Obama's pastor at Trinity UCC in Chicago, the Reverend Wright. Powerful emotions erupting all over the place! Not sure where I am in all of this, but I see no need for a pastor to use the words he does in conveying his thoughts and feelings against this country.

Is Obama becoming a serious candidate for the presidency? I believe the answer has to be yes. Whoever the candidates are, we must pray and then pray some more.

WEDNESDAY, APRIL 30TH

Holy, holy, holy! Lord God Almighty! Early in the morning our song shall rise to thee. It is so very important to begin each day with worship.

Today, my parents, Charles and Marian (Walradth), would have been married seventy-six years. They made thirty-five before my father's death. When they were married, he was nineteen and she was eighteen. He had just graduated from Huntsville High School in Randolph County, Indiana. She used to joke about them being two young love birds!

He had six younger sisters: Mary Elizabeth, Erma Ella, Arletta Marie, Marjorie Louise, Patty Lou, and Judith Ann. All married and had families. A younger brother, Delma Vernon, died at the age of ten. Both Erma (nursing) and Marjorie (elementary education) graduated from Ball State.

She had one younger sister, Glendabell, and three younger brothers: Berl Eli (Deed) and Verl Isaac (Buss) were twins; and Robert Wayne, who became a high school basketball star. All married and had families. Deed (business education) graduated from Ball Sate.

Grateful for the ecumenical correspondence across the nation and occasionally from abroad. Exciting and inspiring!

MAY
2 0 0 8

THURSDAY, MAY 1ST

Rise up, O men of God! The Church for you doth wait, her strength unequal to her task; rise up, and make her great.

Throughout my pastorates I have cried out to God for more men to take the Church seriously. That still remains on my heart and in my soul. Men were given the essential responsibility and authority for Christ's Body, the Church.

Preparation was given to the Rotary Memorial Service for Sunday. It is for the entire district and I am trusting God for its success.

Sometimes it is in service clubs where men really shine. They seem to feel less inhibited. What does that say about the Church in terms of flesh and blood relationships?

I sometimes deeply feel my greatest transitional years were at little Salem Community Church UMC (1985–1987) near Lakes of the Four Seasons and Valparaiso. I had just passed fifty years of age and moved more strongly into an Anglican and Roman Catholic mode of thinking and doing.

FRIDAY, MAY 2ND

Teach us, O Lord, time is Your creation and You are not subject to it. Teach us, O Lord, that humans are!

My trip to Borders in Bloomington, Indiana was safe and sound. It is truly amazing the people I meet. Sales were below average.

Perused a devotional book given to my father more than forty years ago by Uncle Hopkins Kleihauer (UMC pastor in Chicago). Under the reading for January 4th (my birth date), Dad had underlined, "Be faithful, and I will give you the crown of life."

Great memories of the feature story Katie Merlie did on me and my literary ministry in *The Indianapolis Star* (October 2007). Picture taken at Barnes and Noble in Plainfield, Indiana.

I pray every morning for that little band of ecumenists that agreed to be a part of my ecumenical pilgrimage.

SATURDAY, MAY 3RD

My Utmost for His Highest by Oswald Chambers is so refreshing and yet demanding. Thank You, Lord, for these spiritual insights—yes, and to his wife, who made the book possible!

Traveled to the Holiday Inn at the Pyramids in Indianapolis for the district Rotary meeting. Senator Richard G. Lugar was speaker.

Just before noon, went to Borders in Greenwood, Indiana for book signing. Manager John Thompson is always supportive. One of the employees reminded me the Holy Spirit is everywhere!

Grateful for newspaper folks, past and present, at *The Star Press* (Muncie): Larry Lough, John Carlson, Jeanine Lake, Debra Sorrel, Bobbi Walker, Eddie Satterfield, and Rita (Affert) Winters.

Returned to Holiday Inn late to prepare for Sunday memorial service that I am leading. Jim Graham is the district governor of Rotary.

SUNDAY, MAY 4TH

Dear Lord, I miss my personal kneeler and private time in worship at home. Yet, please keep stretching me!

Small crowd at memorial service. However, the focus and outpouring of emotion for deceased Rotarians were a magnificent sight to behold! There were many tears shed for those who have gone to meet their Maker during the year. It was a unique spiritual experience. Much conversation afterward. Many compliments for my handling of the service. I give all credit to the dear Lord!

Went to Natalie's birthday party at Martha and Jeff's. She is three. What a beautiful time it was! Natalie is a very special little girl and Grandpa loves her dearly.

How I have longed for a denomination of substance, depth, and serious spiritual sensitivity.

The early Christians prayed for the dead. Why should we, in our day and time, do anything less?

MONDAY, MAY 5TH

Lord Jesus, fount of mercy and love, please forgive me for all of my sins. Lord, they strike me as grievous and certainly unacceptable.

Isn't it amazing how you and I never get big enough or holy enough that repentance is no longer needed?

Much respect for Father Ernest Falardeau's books (autographed) on the Eucharist. Two, in particular, come to mind: *One Bread and One Cup* and *A Holy and Living Sacrifice*. Long active in ecumenical work at all levels of the Church, he has been a friend and part of my Associates network for many years. He is currently based in New York City.

In a way, we United Methodists are only two steps from Catholicism. To prove the point, we only need to read Charles Wesley's *The Eucharistic Hymns*.

Sometimes the so-called non-canonical books are worthy and profitable. Take Ecclesiasticus, also known as Sirach for example.

TUESDAY, MAY 6TH

Blest be the tie that binds our hearts in Christian love. Indeed, how spiritually delightful it is!

Reflected on my years at Meadowdale UMC, adjacent to Northwest High School in Indianapolis, from 1981 to 1985. These were decisive in my approach to ministry. More and more ecumenical ministry came to the forefront. I became virtually an unpaid staff member of the Indiana Council of Churches. The appointment to a particular church became far less important. A multifaceted ministry of my own with God's help moved permanently into place.

However, remembering affectionately in that church Steve and Donna Casterline, Mike Johnson, Marjorie Graham, Roy and Bonnie Karst, Russ Dozier, John Tice, and Mark Dicken.

Why does so much of life appear to be political expediency? Only God is wise enough to sort that out!

The mafia mentality is not confined to the mob. We clergy can, upon occasion, degenerate into that mode!

WEDNESDAY, MAY 7TH

O God, during the storms of daily living, we are called in faith to rest assured peace will come. Strengthen us in our faith.

Rotary meeting in New Castle delightful and at times hilarious. The scheduled speaker couldn't be there, so some of our members spoke.

It was a relief to transfer money from special funds so we could do major maintenance on our property. We have now owned it five years.

Spent relaxing evening, eating out and walking. Benefits of retirement are to be appreciated, dear Lord. Remind me!

O Lord, keep me ever grateful for good health and ample financial resources. Grant I would be a faithful steward of both.

THURSDAY, MAY 8TH

The Spirit God has given us does not make us timid. Actually, His Spirit fills us with power, love, and self-control.

Thank You, Lord, for the blessings of this life—some I know about and others I don't. Anyway, thank You!

Remembered the elderly priest at Walkerton, Anthony Letko, who used to treat me to lunch at the Notre Dame Club. Jan Blazi, Lou Holtz's secretary, would join us.

My Roman Catholic friends have been many, O Lord. Thank You for them and the gifts they have given me.

Such friends have been and are influential in my spiritual formation. Some of my Protestant colleagues don't know what they are missing!

FRIDAY, MAY 9TH

O Lord, only in You is there security, now and forever. Please continue to impress this on my heart, mind, and soul.

Left early for Tree of Life Bookstore in Marion to leave books for next Friday's signing. Inviting store with a friendly coffee shop.

Made my way, then, to Borders in Mishawaka. When I arrived, table was all set up, ready to go. I really appreciated that. Signing went well.

Delighted to remember what colleague Don Carpenter (UMC) said upon hearing me preach in May of 2005. He said I had just the right combination of scholarship and folksiness.

Returned home before midnight. Thank You, Lord, for those many safe miles. I really count on You!

SATURDAY, MAY 10TH

Jesus is the light of the world and yet the vast majority of people live in darkness. This is a mystery to me, O Lord, but I must not be judgmental of them.

Headed for new Family Christian Book Store in Greenwood. The manager was on top of things, so we went to work right away. Sold five copies in less than thirty minutes. Then, spent most of five hours selling twelve more copies!

Reflected on how the distribution of my published material has begun to change. Sometimes, hands-on is better than a faraway distribution center that can mess up things!

Gave God the glory for my successes and look forward to more challenges. The Holy Spirit continually pushes me into change.

A lot of pain and anger among people today. In a way, there has been for a long, long time. I suspect our affluence has taken its toll!

SUNDAY, MAY 11TH

Mother's Day and Pentecost on the same Sunday! O God, I give thanks for mothers and the coming of the Holy Spirit.

Worshipped at Saint Andrew Presbyterian Church. Clerk of the session asked me to guest preach in June and I agreed.

I suspect, if the sacrifices of really good mothers could have saved the world, it would have been saved a long time ago!

Hail Mary, full of grace, the Lord is with you. Blessed are you among women and blessed is the fruit of your womb, Jesus.

Recalled how badly I wanted to get a sermon published very early in my ministry. Had local printer in 1962 in Greenfield, Indiana print several copies and mailed them out. It was titled, "Four Blessed Events."

MONDAY, MAY 12TH

The gift of your grace, O Lord, is beyond my comprehension. I remember the supreme sacrifice of your Son and am filled with joy.

I beg of You to keep me ever humble and obedient before Your throne. In spite of my gross imperfections, thank You for loving and caring for me.

Father William Treacy's personally autographed copy of *Wild Branch of the Olive Tree* is a prized gift. He is known internationally for his Jewish-Christian dialogue ministry.

Spent some time in the Muncie Mall, reading and observing people. No wonder those of us who write have a lot to say!

As we settle in for the night, please protect grandchildren Natalie Rene and Justin Daniel, who are little and fragile. Grant watchful care, Lord.

TUESDAY, MAY 13TH

Dear God, You have made me such an independent soul! I beg of You that such independence is in harmony with the Holy Spirit.

Motored to Holy Trinity Episcopal Church in South Bend for Indiana Partners for Christian Unity and Mission servant board meeting. Good folks . . . struggling. Pondered the nearly five hours we spent together. Dear Lord, is ecumenism alive and well in Indiana? Yes, Lord, Your will and ways don't fit into mine!

Continue to give thanks for the trip to Saint Stephen's Episcopal Church in Providence, Rhode Island in October of 2007. I had been recommended by someone in the ESBVM in England. I gave a Sunday evening formal presentation on the Blessed Virgin Mary with dialogue following. It seemed to be a very positive event with strong interest. Father John D. Alexander was gracious and affirming. Great event and experience!

When in a negative and defeatist mood, quietly and unhurriedly count your blessings.

In affirmation and appreciation of my father's years as a licensed Congregational-Christian minister, I have wondered about my decision to be a Methodist clergyman.

WEDNESDAY, MAY 14TH

O Lord, keep me ever dependent on You. Grant I would not seek competence apart from Your Holy Spirit.

Truly celebrative day at New Castle Rotary with the recognition of twenty-seven junior Rotarians who had been guests of the club during the year. John Newby, superintendent of schools, made the presentations. This club has done excellent—even exciting—ministry for youth over the years. I am privileged and very grateful to be its president this year.

Reflected on the wonderful, inspirational youth camping program of which I was a part for several years at Epworth Forest in North Webster, Indiana. UMC pastors, churches, and adult leaders aided untold numbers of youth in their development. The experiences were solidly enriching and prepared teens for a wholesome future. Many youth were called to full-time ministry and the benefits of the program are probably beyond measurement.

The Holy Spirit tells me I am "teachable, lovable, and hopeful." Well, that should last me for awhile!

Wake up, O men and women of God, His precious and holy blood cleanses our own impurities.

THURSDAY, MAY 15TH

O Lover of our souls, keep us confident in Your love. When we stray, pull us back and draw us close to You.

Attended Religion Communicators Council at Interchurch Center in Indianapolis. Surprisingly, the program held little interest for much of anyone.

Headed toward New Castle for an evening speaking engagement at the Lions Club. Meeting was moved to a different restaurant without my knowledge, but I eventually found it with the help of Gene Lacy.

Continue to give thanks for UMC colleague Riley Case, a strong evangelical leader. As one of our associates, I find him a spiritually strong fellow with theological expertise which is highly respected in northern Indiana and beyond.

Some would say I have spent most of my life with women. In view of the fact that I have a wife, four daughters, and most of my parishioners have been of the female gender, I would tend to agree!

FRIDAY, MAY 16TH

God will take care of you, through every day, o'er all the way. At my age, you cannot say otherwise . . . the proof is there.

Went to Tree of Life Bookstore in Marion. Signing was slow but fruitful. People were friendly. Those coming and going were more open than I expected. I didn't pick up any negative fundamentalism.

Gave thanks again for Darrel Radford, former managing editor of *The New Castle Courier-Times*. He was so helpful in many ways. This was especially true in putting together my two recent books: *Fast Food for the Soul* and *More Fast Food for the Soul*.

Sometimes it is difficult for me to wait on others for help, Lord. My impatience pushes me to act before it is necessary.

Give thanks that we can overcome evil with good because the Holy Spirit is capable in all situations. Just don't try to control the timing or the way it will happen.

SATURDAY, MAY 17TH

From everlasting to everlasting, Thou are God. Apart from You, O God, we are nothing and have no hope.

Went to Dunkirk (Indiana) High School Alumni banquet. I taught there from 1956 to 1958 and then entered theological seminary. It was a truly inspirational evening! I met several former students and sold many copies of my books with half of the proceeds going back to the alumni association. Those former students I especially remember meeting were John Nieman, Orval Huffman, and Pat Urmon. They were celebrating their fiftieth anniversary of graduating from high school. Fred Beeson, a former teaching colleague, was also present. Dorothy joined me for this joyful occasion and enjoyed visiting with Harry (Tony) Meier. The evening was a high moment.

Reflecting on how difficult it was for me to leave teaching and enter theological seminary, but it was very clear that was what God intended.

Perhaps the most remarkable story I have ever read has to do with salvation history.

I just love the Hail Mary. Sometimes I say it often during the day and even at night.

SUNDAY, MAY 18TH

Learn to call on God both day and night. Be ever watchful of your conduct and pray for the Holy Spirit's continual presence.

Worshipped at First UMC in Anderson. John Wortinger preached a quality sermon that was worthy of publication.

Convinced the United Methodist appointive system never utilized my expertise in homiletics and talents in preaching to the extent it could have. While this has caused some sorrow, it has not throttled or diminished my passion for this imperative pulpit ministry. Consequently, I found other avenues for expression.

With gratitude, I surveyed my high school graduating class of 1950. We went to Center School in Perry Township of Delaware County, Indiana. It is now part of a consolidation called Wapahani. The boys in the class were: Charles O. Jordan, Bob Conwell, Gene Warner, George Windmiller, Curt Buchanan, Thayer Jordan, Dennis Conner (GED), and myself. The girls were: Janet Thornburg, Barbara McKinsey, Phyllis Chalfant, Alice Monroe, Lucretia Mann, Bonnie Warner, Betty Warner, Pat Burleson, and Anita Oxley. Thankful for all of them!

Is it possible for our nation to move toward a purged, renewed, and legitimate paternalism that is servant-oriented?

MONDAY, MAY 19TH

Unless we become like children, we will never enter the Kingdom of Heaven. O God, please teach us the difference between childlike and childish!

Visited with Lamar Imes on the phone for a time. He is now a retired UMC minister, living near Marion. He was a student of mine in the Redkey, Indiana school system. He served as a district superintendent twice as a clergy member of the North Indiana Conference of the UMC. Needless to say, I have been very proud of him all these years. I also had Lamar's wife,

Joan Brenner, in school at Dunkirk. Those teaching years in both schools were and are highly valued and memorable.

My dear wife said that if I had just stayed with one thing, I could have been a success! What can I say, except that my interests have never been confined and focused solely in one field.

In the time in which I have lived, I believe the greatest men have been Sir Winston Churchill and Pope John Paul II. They continually inspire me.

As we have moved about, Dorothy has been such a trooper. She once told our daughters that home is where you hang your hat!

TUESDAY, MAY 20TH

Dear Lord, please grant me the strength, energy, and patience to be and to do all You have provided. I kneel before Your greatness.

Sometimes in our spiritual journey, we think we have lost our way, only to discover the unpleasant detour was planned for our good and the good of others.

I took Dorothy to Sharon's in Fishers and they worked together in a housekeeping venture. Sharon's apartment was in need!

I spent time mailing newsletters, visiting people, promoting my books, and buying a new pair of shoes.

We returned and spent a relaxing evening watching television. Hillary was winning Kentucky and Obama was winning Oregon. They are the last major primaries.

WEDNESDAY, MAY 21ST

Lord, keep me humble and sensitive to Your holy will. Grant those persons and situations in which I find myself are conducive to everyone's growth.

Rotary meeting was good news/bad news. Speaker had quality ideas but spoke far too long. Board was productive, as usual.

When former Bishop A. James Armstrong resigned from the UMC Indiana area, it broke my heart. He held so much promise for us. In a way, it was a tragedy that lingers in my memory.

Somewhat at loose ends, so I spent considerable time reading and reflecting from *The Imitation of Christ* by Thomas A. Kempis. It is a spiritually powerful book which speaks to one's depth. More specifically, at times, it enables us to get a glimpse of our sometimes sorry souls!

Believe Methodism is regaining a belief in the real presence of the Lord's Supper. Praise God!

THURSDAY, MAY 22ND

O Lamb of God, who takes away the sins of the world, have mercy! Lord Jesus, through Your death we are made right with the Father.

Sought to bring several matters up-to-date. If only we knew when to throw away our correspondence, etc.

My wife and I painted the garage door. It is the best looking one in the subdivision! After living in parsonages for more than forty years, owning a home is quite an experience.

The future beckons and God is by my side, but I must have faith. Faith and works go together. Christians, are you listening?

O God, please forgive me for any heartache I may have caused this day. Melt my heart and keep my mind focused on You.

FRIDAY, MAY 23RD

Speak, Lord . . . speak, Lord . . . speak, Lord. Your servant is listening, Lord. He is listening, Lord. He is listening, Lord.

Mostly a day of perusing materials. Sometimes I think I should write an autobiography of thousands of pages! But, who would read it?

Memorial Day is upon us. I pray often for the Walradths and the Lacys, granting none would be lost in eternity—those who have gone on . . . those who remain . . . those yet to come.

We need healing, Lord, individually and as a nation. I beg of You to come with Your healing powers and spiritually restore us.

A lengthy walk alone provided time for reflecting and looking into the future. Lord, Your servant is listening.

SATURDAY, MAY 24TH

One day at a time, sweet Jesus! Whether by country music or choral mass, our sweet Jesus is ever with us.

We joined our family for the Indianapolis 500 Parade in the downtown area. What a beautiful and enjoyable experience! Everyone was present, except son-in-law Jeffrey and grandson Justin Daniel. It seemed better for father to babysit. Son-in-law Terry Beyl's parents also came along. They are Bill and Jo Beyl of New Albany, Indiana. I have discovered Bill and Jo to be genuinely good people. He is a retired school administrator. Terry is their only child.

I am not much of a racing fan, but I arrived home with a feeling that my day was well spent. Proud of Indiana's prominence in an area of international interest.

Our young people have such complicated lives today with temptations virtually by the hour. Yet, that does not excuse them from seeking to live out the ideals of the Christian life.

When the Holy Spirit presides in a worship service, I am humbly elated and shout praises to God, the Father!

SUNDAY, MAY 25TH

Life is so precious, dear Lord. You have blessed me too many ways for me to count and I am humbled. In good times and bad times and all in between, You have loved me.

Worshipped at Central Christian in Anderson. The experience was inspiring and invigorating. The pastor is a very talented fellow.

J. Russell Townsend Jr. (Indianapolis businessman and former Indiana state legislator) was a consistent supporter of my ecumenical network.

The Indianapolis 500 race was much in the air. There will be hundreds of thousands of people there and so vulnerable. Grant Your protective powers, Lord.

In the evening, an enjoyable drive was taken to the Prairie Creek Reservoir, southeast of Muncie. My Grandfather Walradth owned some of that land, now covered by water.

MONDAY, MAY 26TH

The Lord is my Shepherd; I shall not want. O great Shepherd of the sheep, please care for hurting others and tell them You love them.

Being a pastor is a distinct privilege. Doors open for us that do not open for others. Yes, and secrets are shared that, at times, can be tumultuous. Keep Your pastors and priests ever faithful, dear Lord!

It was a day of little activity because of being a legal holiday. The dead were remembered across our land. Praise God!

While the war in Iraq is generally unpopular, our service men and women are honored with genuine respect.

Precious Lord, hold our hands in the United States of America. We beg for Your forgiveness and a new day of national and personal morality.

TUESDAY, MAY 27TH

Give thanks to the Lord, for He is good; his love endures forever. The psalmist tells it like it is!

A fruitful day of correspondence. It seems some days like there is so much to do and so little time to do it . . . even in retirement.

Paused to think and give thanks for Sister Agnes Louise Paulus, now deceased, of Marian College in Fond du Lac, Wisconsin. She invited me to do a keynote address on the Blessed Virgin Mary at the college about twenty years ago. It was truly a memorable day. She wrote dozens of letters to me over the years and was always very affirming. She said I reminded her of John Henry Cardinal Newman! As Methodist and Catholic, we shared our love for Mother Mary.

I pray everyday for every congregation and constituency I have served. I do so with gratitude.

The sixth chapter of John says it very well in verse 53: "I am telling you the truth: if you do not eat the flesh of the Son of Man and drink his blood, you will not have life in yourselves" (TEV).

WEDNESDAY, MAY 28TH

Rescue the perishing, care for the dying, Jesus is merciful, Jesus will save. When I was a small boy, these are some of the first words I remember.

In today's world, there seems to be little sense of being lost in the spiritual sense. Is hell no longer a reality? Are we all going to heaven? Is there no hereafter?

Rotary went smoothly. I announced we had received nine new members this year, beginning from July 1, 2007. Loud applause followed! It is definitely a stronger club than it was a year ago. Perhaps my contribution was setting the stage for this to happen. My style is that of being pastoral.

O Lord, there are so many opportunities in this life. How do I make use of all of them? I try, Lord, but please be patient. Regardless, help me always to be spiritual in every situation.

Virtually everything I know about this world moves in direct or indirect opposition to our Lord. Well, yes, we are aliens.

THURSDAY, MAY 29TH

Be ever mindful of the life God has given to you and only you. Be careful to celebrate it and give glory for its uniqueness.

Personal business was a top priority with the writing of checks and doing other necessities to make life flow smoothly.

Sometimes I wonder to how many different hospitals across Indiana and beyond I have made pastoral calls. Among my favorites were Deaconess in Evansville, Saint Joseph's Medical Center in South Bend, Saint Vincent in Indianapolis, Ball Memorial in Muncie, and Methodist in Indianapolis.

Recalled Dorothy's twelve-day stay in 2005 at Ball Memorial. I took her to the emergency room on our anniversary (November 6th).

Represented Rotary Club at Bundy Auditorium in New Castle to present our scholarships to graduates. The community is to be congratulated for the numerous awards given by many organizations.

FRIDAY, MAY 30TH

Praise be to the One Who died for us and arose again from the dead. His salvation is more precious than all the world's valuables.

Left before 5:00 AM to go to annual conference in West Lafayette, Indiana. The meetings are actually at Purdue University.

Ate breakfast with Christian Unity Committee in Purdue's Union Building. Excellent meeting with strong interest.

Did book signing for Cokesbury. It was a very stimulating event. I saw several old friends and believe made some new ones. Sold many books and returned home with much satisfaction. So grateful I have lived this long and remained productive.

The clerical collar has a way of simply saying I understand myself in a priestly way and summoned to be holy.

SATURDAY, MAY 31ST

Help us to sing of Your love everyday, O Lord. It is in You we discover all that matters and ever will!

Remembered living in homes close to Ball State campus during my junior (North Martin) and senior (Tillotson) years. A couple of fellows come to mind who roomed in the same houses I did: Larry Buell from Rolling Prairie, Indiana who entered politics and became an Indiana state legislator and Bill May from Hagerstown, Indiana who became a widely known basketball referee at the state level and beyond.

Dorothy and I went to Fishers to visit Martha and the children. Jeff had to be in Cincinnati with his new law firm (Taft, Stettinius & Hollister). Since my retirement in 2003, so much of major importance has happened. In particular, we have two new grandchildren!

While some goals fall by the wayside, new and just as significant experiences come into being. God is always ahead of us!

Often it seems, unless promotion, power and money are at hand, ecumenism will have few devotees.

JUNE
2 0 0 8

SUNDAY, JUNE 1ST

O Lord God, Lamb of God, remind us daily of Your love that always seeks our good. Please forgive our doubts and lead us to wherever You want.

We worshipped at Saint Andrew Presbyterian. I felt so sorry for the pastor, who became ill and couldn't finish the service. It might have happened to anyone of us in the clergy!

Dorothy and I enjoyed ourselves in one of Muncie's restaurants and returned home to our projects.

Wrote my column for *The Star Press*. It dealt with showbiz religion and its deficiency in meeting our deeper basic needs. So many stars and starlets seem to have fallen by the wayside!

Continued to appreciate those who visited with me at Cokesbury book signing during annual conference. I did miss the presence of an old friend, Bill Cross, former manager. We had worked together for at least thirty years.

MONDAY, JUNE 2ND

Remember, Lord, when I used to walk the fields as a new teenager and dream of the future? Yes, You were there!

I have been aware of God's presence as far back as I can recall. The call to the ordained ministry really began about the age of thirteen.

Purchased wafers and kosher wine for Holy Communion. The Lord called me to these daily private Eucharists in 1985.

Enjoyed some time just loafing and being thankful, especially for a matter being resolved over the phone.

Your grace, O Lord, is so powerful and loving. I do believe it can fix anything and/or anyone! Thank You.

TUESDAY, JUNE 3RD

Lord, have mercy. Christ, have mercy. Lord, have mercy. Please minister to those who are downtrodden and abused.

Ate lunch at Bob Evans in Anderson with representative from Indiana Christian Chamber of Commerce. Enlightening! So much is going on that is truly good outside of regular denominational channels. He was very helpful in bringing me in touch with independent groups.

Once again relished the creative book Janice Emshwiller put together for Dorothy and me. She calls herself Raggedy Jan and is a member of Trinity UMC in Hartford City, Indiana. God bless her.

Jon Gosser, new chair of the Christian Unity Committee of the NIC, much on my mind. Trusting in the Holy Spirit. His father, Dave, was also a UMC pastor.

Watched on television Obama's delegate count go beyond number needed for nomination. Who will be his running mate? Probably a surprise.

WEDNESDAY, JUNE 4TH

Our Blessed Lord says He will never leave us or forsake us. That is what He means and we are to believe it!

Attended retired UMC breakfast here in Muncie. Large crowd and good chemistry among people, who delighted me.

Rotary meeting small in numbers. A major storm had gone through the area last night. Another excellent program.

Did personal banking in New Castle. Grateful to learn one of the tellers had cut out one of my newspaper columns and put it on her bulletin board.

A relaxing evening in Muncie Mall. My wife and I ate at MCL and visited with Hope Barnes, widow of former UMC pastor.

THURSDAY, JUNE 5TH

Every day is a good day to be celebrated. Why? Because Jesus the Christ is our Savior and Lord . . . now and forever.

Prepared for two book signings, one in Bloomington and another in Lafayette. Especially hoping the Bloomington event will be fruitful, even above and beyond number of books sold!

John Nieman, one of my former students at Dunkirk (Class of 1958), came by and left a framed photograph from *The News Sun*. John, among others, was a prize pupil during my teaching years at the two neighboring towns of Dunkirk and Redkey in Jay County, Indiana. He has a winsome personality that makes him tend to stand out above others.

I give thanks daily for a life that has now gone into its seventy-fifth year. Generally good health and ample financial resources are deeply appreciated. I have lived twenty years longer than my father. I am grateful for everything and everyone.

Worked on my sermon for next Sunday. Will focus on the imperative and serious nature of our Faith.

FRIDAY, JUNE 6TH

Remind me again and again, O Lord, that You will never leave me nor forsake me. My fears are sometimes real and my faith needs strengthening.

Left before 6:00 AM to go to Bloomington and the South Indiana Conference to sign books. For some reason, generally, books were not selling easily. Visited with Marsha Tucker Hutchinson, a staff member of Saint Luke's UMC in Indianapolis. Her parents were in a former church I pastored. They were Tom and Pansy Tucker. Tom was a Buick dealer on North Keystone. The church was Union Chapel UMC, located near Keystone at the Crossing in Indianapolis.

Visited with Mark Dicken, among other clergy, who had been a member of the other Indianapolis church I served, Meadowdale/Northwest UMC. He was a practicing attorney and briefly my pastor/parish chair there. Mark has now been a successful UMC pastor for some years.

Recalled two boyhood friends, Noel Burton and Milford Cross. Noel became a CPA and Milford spent several years in the military.

How can we possibly remember all of the people who have made contributions to our lives? Obviously, we can't, but we must try and name them!

SATURDAY, JUNE 7TH

More love to Thee, O Christ, more love to Thee! Forgive our frailty, O Christ, as we seek to love You in Your entirety.

Off to Lafayette for a signing at Family Christian Book Store. Storms were in the area, so the travel was not smooth. Met by book store manager and made to feel at home. He was generous and cooperative in style. It went well. Flowed with smoothness and was not blighted by extremes of feast or famine.

Regardless of the criticisms of the USA, we are still much a land of opportunity and freedom of religious expression is certainly to be accentuated. We are to be reminded of what we waste, especially food!

How many of us, even in the clergy, sacrifice to any extent? Yes, God's people can be spoiled!

Celebrated on the way home and thanked God for everything and everyone. A new venue had opened and more potential was obvious.

SUNDAY, JUNE 8TH

O Master, let me walk with Thee. Let me do so in lowly paths of service free. Tell me Thy secret!

Preached at Saint Andrew Presbyterian and was warmly received. I really need to preach more. My doctorate was in homiletics!

My wife and I shared a delicious buffet at Ruby Tuesday's. If we move from our present location, we will miss the good eating places that are close.

Headed for Walkerton, Indiana to join the graduation and celebration of Emma Jane Hostetler. She is unusually precious.

Trip to Walkerton and back consumed five hours or so, but it was worth every mile to share those moments with the Hostetler family, former parishioners.

MONDAY, JUNE 9TH

Onward Christian soldiers! That battle cry has been heard in many forms throughout the centuries. It remains our Christian command.

Gave thanks for all of my appointments in Indiana. After supplying churches from 1957 to 1959 (Spartansburg, Spiceland, and Webster), I became a resident pastor from 1959 to 2003.

Churches served were Philadelphia (near Greenfield), Trinity Kokomo, Muncie College Avenue (Associate), Hagerstown (near Richmond), and Union Chapel, Indianapolis.

Followed by Saint James East Evansville (now McCutchanville), Seymour First, Princeton First (now Hillside), Saint Paul's Rushville, and Meadowdale (now Northwest) Indianapolis.

Followed by Salem (near Valparaiso), Leesburg (near Warsaw), Battle Ground (near Lafayette), Argos (near Plymouth), Walkerton (near South Bend), and Yorktown (near Muncie).

TUESDAY, JUNE 10TH

Forever, O Lord, I shall cling to You. Only in You can I put my complete trust. Please grant Your mercy . . . always.

I served sixteen different churches as a resident pastor in forty-four years, averaging just under three years. Ironically, I worked for twenty-eight different district superintendents over the same period!

They were: A. Wesley Pugh, Bob Yunker, Gerald Jones, Thurman Morris, John Sayre, Virgil Siberal, L. G. Sapp, K. K. Merryman, Mark Blaising, and Charles Tyler.

Followed by David Lawson (bishop, deceased), Charles Myers, Bob DeLong, Howard Rogers, Willard Doyle, Charles Armstrong, Charles Ballard, Sam Phillips, Jim Babbitt, and Tom Rough.

Followed by J. Wilbur Yates, Louis Haskell, Mike Coyner (now bishop), Susan Messenger, Walter Mayer, Lamar Imes, Jack Hartman, and David Maish.

WEDNESDAY, JUNE 11TH

Help us, dear Lord, to see ourselves the way You see us. There is so much about us we just don't understand!

Reflecting on yesterday's early morning breakfast with brother Mike. It has begun to be a mutually supportive relationship and I am grateful.

Splendid Rotary Club meeting that honored ten teachers in the New Castle School System. Gene Lacy did an inspirational job with the presentations.

While I was at Hagerstown, Everett Ferrill offered me a fellowship to do a doctorate at Ball State. We had four little girls and such a move would never have worked.

Much appreciated invitations over a period of years to preach in the chapel at Anderson University. Professional staff is always welcoming and supportive.

THURSDAY, JUNE 12TH

Grant Your peace, O Lord. I never want peace as the world gives it, but the superior quality that lasts forever.

Morning coffee with a friend in the banking business Stan Schad. He is a very personable man I met in Yorktown.

Friendships that are meaningful and durable are few. Acquaintances for those in the pastoral ministry are numerous and often surface relationships.

Remembered ecumenically oriented UMC pastors—friends for many years. Three are Ed Johnson (Wisconsin), Paul Perry (Texas, now deceased), and Ron Yonker (South Carolina).

Motivate me and enable me, dear Lord, to be a better friend to others. I need to be more open to those you send me.

FRIDAY, JUNE 13TH

Thrill us with Your Holy Spirit, Lord! Motivate us to higher heights in harmony with Your Holy Spirit.

A day of setting up new book signings and much pondering about the past, present, and future. Work to be done!

Remembered ecumenical colleagues of bygone years: Beverly A. Nitschke (Lutheran), Waneda Baker (UMC), David F. Rees (Lutheran), and Bishop Ted Jones (Episcopalian).

It strains my memory to account even for most of them I knew so well. Monsignor Ray Bosler (RC) was a delightful fellow and humorous.

Yes, and there were Cato Petry (Church of the Brethren), Dr. Robert Brown (UMC), Frank E. Tolbert (Episcopalian), and Sister Ancilla Dwyer (RC).

SATURDAY, JUNE 14TH

Love, perfect love. That reflects the yearning of humanity. We Christians see dimly and we must be thankful for that.

Went to do a book signing at Tree of Life Bookstore in Greenwood. It was my first time there and I had to search for the location. In a way, it was a mom and pop store, solely owned by a husband and wife team. This was different and refreshing. Signing went well, folks were kind and a healthy spirit prevailed. So pleased that was the environment, which is not always the case!

Discovering the south side of Indianapolis and somewhat beyond is satisfying and at the same time challenging. Thank You, Lord.

As we survey our lives, it is remarkable how much we have learned and many of us by now should be far better people than we were thirty or forty years ago.

Praise God, from Whom all blessings flow. The one, holy, catholic apostolic Church gives Christ's people a home here and now. We are called to come home and stay there!

SUNDAY, JUNE 15TH

Everyday we have, O Lord, is one of celebration. Remind us gently or firmly, Lord, to be grateful for all of them.

Went to worship at Fishers UMC. Our grandson Justin Daniel was baptized by Michael Reed the pastor. Well handled! Pictures were taken and we all celebrated. All of our little family was there, except Sharon, who had to work.

Then, we enjoyed a noon meal together at Bob Evans. It took some doing, but all of us (nine) were able to sit together. It was truly a happy occasion.

It was also a time of celebrating Father's Day as well. I received inspiring cards, plus gift cards and a check.

All four of our daughters were baptized by United Methodist ministers. The only one I baptized was Anne Marie.

MONDAY, JUNE 16TH

Please continue Your work in me, Holy Spirit—yes, and with me, through me, and for me. Truly, this is abundant life.

A morning of solid accomplishment in my study, especially thank-you notes and checks written.

My Chicago Cubs are doing well this year. How good the team is remains to be seen. I remember the last time they were in the World Series (1945). That team's stars were: Phil Cavaretta, Stan Hack, Hank Borowy, Hank Wyse, Bill Nicholson, Andy Pafko. Detroit Tigers beat them in that series, four to three.

Called Father Thomas Murphy at Hermitage House in Beech Grove, Indiana, but he is unable to be visited this week. I do believe his condition is worsening. He is a great ecumenical friend and colleague.

The priesthood has been and is of special interest to me. I find meaning and fascination in it, whether it be Roman Catholic, Anglican, or Orthodox.

TUESDAY, JUNE 17TH

Keep us ever humble and obedient, Lord. Your glory is what counts. All beginnings and endings are with You.

Spent most of the day working on newsletter materials for my Associates. *The Wall Street Journal* is always an excellent source.

Greatly concerned about our nation. We have traveled roads of gross immorality for so long, it is hard to see the cliff just ahead.

Call us individually and collectively to repentance, O Lord. Tragedy is not far away and it may come like a thief in the night.

As faithful Christians, we give thanks for Your ongoing grace. Dear Lord, I thank You from the bottom of my heart.

WEDNESDAY, JUNE 18TH

O Lord, help us to be simple and plain. Grant we would observe children that we may have a strong indication of how to live.

Light crowd at the Rotary meeting, but all seemed satisfied. I only have one more meeting as president. It has been a distinct privilege.

Work in backyard is coming along nicely. We are putting up a much-needed new fence and removing a tree.

So much of television is miscellaneous and sometimes hurtful. Teach me, Lord, to use my time more profitably.

Personal letter from Bishop Higi of the Lafayette Diocese was inspirational. I had given him a gift for the development of the priesthood.

THURSDAY, JUNE 19TH

Continue to mold me into your likeness, O Lord. Grant that I would be Your disciple not merely in appearance, but also in an obvious reality.

What a pleasant and enjoyable day! I began by traveling to downtown Indianapolis and shopping at Krieg's Brothers Religious Supply store. There I bought a new white, short-sleeved Toomey clergy shirt. Mrs. Krieg, an old friend, advised me Father Murphy was seriously ill.

Went to Scottish Rite Cathedral, majestic and magnificent, and visited library. Met a tour guide, Tracy Hutton, a former parishioner at Philadelphia UMC (1959–1962).

Meditated at Christ Cathedral (Episcopal) and had lunch at the Columbia Club for first time in months. Both are on the Circle, which, in some ways, is the center of the Hoosier State.

While alone and yet not alone, it is hard to explain the peace and satisfaction I experienced.

FRIDAY, JUNE 20TH

Be careful how and what you think; your life is shaped by your thoughts. Seek to guard your mind from all impurities.

Reflected on the UMC bishops under whom I ministered for forty-four years plus. A colleague once said to me, upon the changing of bishops, "when the gods change, the rules change!" Some truth to this.

I came into the ministry under Richard C. Raines, a towering Episcopal figure, whom I greatly admired. Rueben Mueller served as a capable unifier of the EUB-Methodist union.

Ralph T. Alton was very relational and I felt a closeness to him that I did not feel for the others. A. James Armstrong was the most brilliant of all, but resigned before his term ended.

Likeable though he be, Leroy Hodapp would have made an outstanding executive secretary of Kiwanis International! Woody White was an astute, kind African American.

SATURDAY, JUNE 21ST

Lord, I need more humility and compassion. Through Your tender mercy, please grant them.

Did first of two book signings at Walden's in Anderson. Slow day. Flow of people mostly minimal. Toward evening, more people began to arrive and more books were sold. Strangely, effects of the International Church of God Convention, which draws thousands, was barely felt. Gave thanks for the precious persons with whom I conversed. Vast majority did not buy books!

Did some light musing about my first automobile. I bought a yellow 1942 Ford soon after graduating from high school with money made while working for Dad and Grandfather (Lacy) in the plastering business. It was one of the few manufactured near the beginning of World War II. It provided transportation for two years from our home to and from Ball State. Then, I sold it to continue my education and moved to a small room in Muncie.

Holy Spirit of God, I want always to be in harmony with You. Do with me what You will, glorifying the Father.

Days and nights come and go for all of humanity. Only God is eternally permanent.

SUNDAY, JUNE 22ND

Praises be to the Father, Son, and Holy Spirit for another special day of worship. O Lord, be with every congregation today.

Worshipped at Muncie High Street UMC. It was the close of their Vacation Bible School. Delightful service! It is a special treat to worship there because of having attended there regularly as a college student in the early 1950s. Eventually baptized and confirmed there by the Rev. Newman Jeffrey in May of 1954. I was a small town, rural boy without sophistication and found a home there. Greatly blessed!

Did second book signing at Walden's in Anderson. Another slow day, but I did sign a copy of *Collected Works* for a Ball State professor.

Our lives seem to change a lot and yet they remain the same! Some day God will explain this to us.

Even for the non-believer, surely he/she is convinced of eternity and the need to pull all loose ends together.

MONDAY, JUNE 23RD

Dear Lord, You have promised never to give us more of a load than we can carry. Thank You for meeting my need.

Worked briefly in my study and then left the remainder of the day for Dorothy and me. We needed some quality time together. Went to a movie and saw Harrison Ford; it was an action move with much mystery. We ate a lot of popcorn! Then, we decided to get something to eat at Burger King. We seldom go to fast food places, but enjoyed it immensely.

I sometimes wonder how other pastors and their wives in retirement are doing. Hopefully, there is enjoyment and a sense of fulfillment.

For many months I have offered a Service of Intercession and Holy Communion for a special person late at night. This time it was for Taylor Burton-Edwards.

TUESDAY, JUNE 24TH

O Lord, teach us once again as a nation the power of repentance and forgiveness. Abortion is all about us and too often we are silent or worse.

Visited Dr. John B. Ashman for my annual eye examination. He is a thorough professional and real gentleman. All came out well at his office. I am grateful, O Lord, and give You all the credit. Please be with those who have poor eyesight or worse.

Worked on my closing prayer for the Rotary meeting tomorrow. We will pray it together.

My wife's health is causing me concern again. Nevertheless, we have been very blessed by her doing as well as she is. Certainly, some of the success is her knowledge of herself.

O great Physician, provide for us in ways we are incapable of doing. We are so limited!

WEDNESDAY, JUNE 25TH

First seek the Kingdom of God and what He requires of you. It is the only way to be in keeping with the Father, Son, and Holy Spirit.

Rotary meeting was very special and brought tears to my eyes. It was the last one of my presidency. Kit Crane, incoming president, presented me with the finest plaque I have ever received during my professional years. He also gave me a very impressive lapel pin. I received a standing ovation from those present and shall be grateful for that the remainder of my life!

It felt so good to be sincerely appreciated. It was important to me this happened in the county (Henry County, Indiana) where I was born.

Service clubs have meant a great deal to me over many years. Their ecumenical composition is almost always positive.

I am reminded we get up doing ministry and go to bed doing ministry. The encompassing nature of our Faith is one of the sure signs of its legitimacy.

THURSDAY, JUNE 26TH

O Lord, please love and care for my family, especially my wife. We are approaching fifty years of marriage and we want to celebrate together!

Called Will Rubach and apologized for not mentioning his name at Rotary yesterday. He did a splendid job of coordinating our meals.

Dorothy and I had the day free, so we headed for Noblesville, Indiana and the new businesses there. Of course, we had fun and food!

Have high hopes for three young men: Matt Goebel, a youth minister in Warsaw, Indiana; Chris Roberts, an associate pastor in Kokomo; and Jason Morris, an associate in suburban Muncie.

Lord, we beg of You to save all of us from a selfish spirit and an attitude of self-sufficiency that thwarts Your will.

FRIDAY, JUNE 27TH

O Father, teach me Your will and ways. Needed improvements in my life are most noticeable.

Headed for Kokomo and a book signing at Books-A-Million. Met Daryl, the manager, who proceeded to make everything available. Signing was well above average. We sold at least twenty-one copies. This event was welcomed and helped to put the Anderson signings in perspective. Of course, God always knows what He is doing!

Recalled with some discomfort how very timid I was as a little boy. I could almost feel physical pain!

I was an only child and the only grandchild on the Walradth side of the house for more than six years. While attention was positively focused on me, so were expectations!

Thank You, Lord, for all Your blessings. Keep me ever humble, obedient, and grateful. Abundant living—yes, Lord!

SATURDAY, JUNE 28TH

Keep speaking to Your servant, Lord. Keep speaking to Your servant, Lord. Grant your will be done and Your ways prevail.

Went to Hastings bookstore in Richmond, Indiana for a signing. It was really a surprising event. Sales were great! Jack and Loretta (Harris) Hatcher came by and bought books. They are CHS graduates (Perry Township, Delaware County, Indiana). Charlie from Webster UMC made a special trip to see me. It had been fifty years since I had supplied his church! I knew his mother well; she was one of the pillars of that little church and very supportive.

Reflected with thanksgiving on my fiftieth anniversary of graduating from Ball State (1954–2004). I was on the social committee, along with my former staff/parish chair from Yorktown UMC, Max Shideler. It was truly a gala occasion with the acting president of BSU, Beverly Pitts, celebrating with us. The alumni office had planned well with several of us.

During my undergraduate days at BSU, I had to look up numerous words and their meanings, which took considerable time. I kept note-books for reference.

Loved my studies with few exceptions at BSU. They virtually became my life.

SUNDAY, JUNE 29TH

Forever, O God, you are my God. You have come to me as Father, Son, and Holy Spirit.

Worshipped at Central Christian in Anderson. It was largely a service of music. People received us readily and warmly. The church is nearing its one hundred fiftieth birthday!

We enjoyed ourselves at the Texas Roadhouse, there in the city. Again, grateful we can do these things. Some years ago, I wondered if I would retire well enough to eat out at all!

Planned projects, especially book signings. Cost of gasoline has become a problem. Well over three dollars per gallon is causing most all of us to look more carefully at our driving.

Deeply in our souls we sense some corrections coming in the way we live our lives. Just what all that entails, of course, only our loving and just God knows.

MONDAY, JUNE 30TH

Lord Jesus, You told Saint Paul Your grace was sufficient for him and Your power is made perfect in weakness. I believe that is meant for all of us.

I visited with an executive at Barnes and Noble in New York City about my books failing to get to distributors and booksellers. Believe problem is solved.

So grateful for the opportunity to present my published materials to the public. More opportunities on the horizon!

Gave thanks for two professional counselors, who were very helpful during mid-career: Foster Williams and Jay Althouse.

Re-read Rudyard Kipling's poem "If." Over a period of years, it was very influential and seemed like Holy Scripture!

JULY
2 0 0 8

TUESDAY, JULY 1ST

Breathe on me breath of God until I am wholly Thine. Heal me with Your powerful love now and forever.

A day of many phone calls and one that was quite a surprise. I was asked to preach and celebrate Holy Communion next Sunday at two churches. The call came from the Rushville, Indiana District Office UMC. I am to be at both New Castle Trinity and Salem. As a retired pastor, I need to be available for such situations that require an elder in the UMC. The invitation was appreciated.

Having some difficulty with posture, walking and headaches. Trusting it is only a natural result of getting older!

Paused to recollect how I used my *Kaltenborn's 1942 War Atlas* to follow the developments of the Second World War. I was a preteen but very interested in the events.

Also paused to recollect my love of both geography and history at an early age that has continued throughout my life.

WEDNESDAY, JULY 2ND

Guide me, O Thou great Jehovah, throughout this barren land. Indeed, O Lord, we are reminded, sometimes painfully, You are not of this world.

Went to New Castle on personal business. Attended Rotary meeting, now as a former president, at the correctional facility. After lunch we took a brief tour that was led by Jeff Wrigley, the warden, who is also a Rotarian. Very informative!

Located the churches where I am to be this Sunday. For the first time in my long pastoral ministry, I will get to serve briefly a two-point charge!

Thank You, Lord, for my financial resources. You have enabled me to have more than enough and I'm most grateful. Keep me humble!

I also remembered with compassion my father's struggles with finances and how he unwillingly became dependent on my grandfather.

THURSDAY, JULY 3RD

There is a balm in Gilead to make the wounded whole. There is a balm in Gilead to heal the sin-sick soul. Thank you, Lord!

Received phone call from David Schwarz of Corinth UMC (near Muncie). He needs me to guest preach at both services on July 20th and I agreed to do so.

Reflected on my pastorate at Leesburg UMC (near Warsaw, Indiana) from 1987–1990. Highlight of those years was a summer Sunday morning lake service on Tippecanoe at Patona Bay. My last year there we broke the three hundred mark in attendance. I preached from a pontoon boat! Our church was the sole sponsor.

There were special people in that church which included Iva Marie Rosbrugh, Sheri Bliele, Wallace Huffman, Millie Paton, Waldo Adams, Rocky and Peggy Cuila, Jim and Claudia Archer, Malcolm Case, Violet Tom, June Vanator, Florence Clark, Robert Bishop Sr., and Al and Norma Hayes.

Waldo Adams was a special intellectual friend and we shared our love for history. When he died, the family delayed the funeral until I returned from vacation.

FRIDAY, JULY 4TH

O Lord, thank You for the United States of America. We are a chosen people and are great because You say so and not because we say so.

Did preparation for Sunday's services and needed correspondence. If I ever receive as much mail as I have sent, the postal box will never hold it!

Did research in both North and South Indiana Conference Journals (UMC). Once it's in your blood, I guess it remains there for a lifetime!

God has blessed me with a long, active ordained ministry and that gives me a perspective which is very helpful. Humanly speaking, a half-century is a long time.

Watched the fireworks from our subdivision. The quality was impressive. It was also surprisingly special and immediately north of us. God bless America!

SATURDAY, JULY 5TH

Your will and Your ways, O Lord. Mold me into the likeness of Jesus the Christ and His apostles, now and forever.

It was an unusual day. Dorothy and I cared for Martha and Jeff's children all day. So, parents were off together to celebrate, shop, and eat. It was their fifth wedding anniversary. They were married at Saint Mary Catholic Church in Indianapolis. I assisted in the service and gave the homily. Felt privileged and grateful.

Their children, Natalie Rene and Justin Daniel, were a light burden. Not so secretly, Grandfather Lacy adores them!

We returned home exhausted and retired early to bed. So pleased with that little family. Their religious faith is precious to them.

As families move through the generations, it is so very important the way be paved with the imperative nature of religious faith. The family trees must not be allowed to wither!

SUNDAY, JULY 6TH

Peace, peace, God's peace. Such contentment is one that passes human understanding and is truly a gift from above.

It was an exceptionally fulfilling day with trips to two churches, providing preaching and Holy Communion. Thanks be to God!

The service at Trinity UMC New Castle was well-handled by the lay leader. I was very kindly and respectfully received.

The service at Salem UMC, near Straughn, had more young people, including two boys, who were acolytes. One parishioner and I discovered our grandmothers were sisters (McCall)!

It was a great joy to share my ordination with those in need. We all seemed to be blessed by the Holy Spirit.

MONDAY, JULY 7TH

Love is patient and kind. Teach me, O Lord, to be more patient and kind. Do for me and others what we cannot do for ourselves.

A catching-up day before I begin on my presentation to the First International ESBVM-USA Congress.

Dorothy and I went to Winchester, Indiana to get her car serviced. It was a fun trip with pie and coffee.

Keeping track of my materials has become a major job, especially as I continue to minister in various ways.

Please forgive me, Lord, for any wrong thoughts I have. Keep me ever open to Your Holy Spirit, Who corrects and purifies.

TUESDAY, JULY 8TH

Before You, O Lord, I kneel in humble adoration. Your wisdom is far beyond mine. I love Your Kingdom.

Began in earnest my paper for the First International ESBVM-USA Congress to be held in Pittsburgh. The Holy Spirit is present. Carefully crafted the introduction and initial four points. Trusting the Holy Spirit will be the real author!

Went to Fishers to pick up daughter Sharon for a couple of days. She seemed delighted to spend some quality time with us.

Pondered my life and wondered about accepting a pastorate again. That will become evident one way or another.

The brevity of life came to me in my fifties. I suspect that is rather typical for most folks.

WEDNESDAY, JULY 9TH

Your grace, O Lord, shower me with Your grace! I beg of You to do for this sinful nation and world what they cannot do for themselves.

Sharon seemed to enjoy herself with a big home-cooked breakfast. She and Dorothy then went shopping and sightseeing in the area.

I went to Rotary in New Castle and greatly enjoyed sitting among those I love. Kit Crane was somewhat nervous, but presided quite well.

Went for my annual physical to Dr. Mark Reedy's office. Even in healthcare, money is an overriding factor.

Please, dear Lord, be with those who provide healthcare. Remind the personnel they really have a ministry to perform and are held accountable.

THURSDAY, JULY 10TH

Time on this earth is so precious, Lord. Help and inspire me to make the best use of it. Thank You for leading me in new areas of service.

We took Sharon to Indianapolis for a day at the zoo. It was warm and sunny. Fortunately, shade was close by. We toured the entire grounds. The variety of creatures was amazing and there was a certain Hoosier pride that came upon me. She enjoyed herself. This was especially true of the meals we provided at home or in the restaurants. She loves to eat and drink, which pleases us!

Keep, O Lord, our little family tight with one another but even more so with You. Help us to remember our sons-in-law come from families of their own and to respect that.

While never much of an athlete, I recalled an eighth grade basketball tournament experience. I made a winning shot for our little school (Center Junior High School, Delaware County) that beat Muncie Wilson Junior High School.

It seems, dear Lord, there is still so much to do in this life. When my work (ministry) is done, I guess You will tell me in definitive terms!

FRIDAY, JULY 11TH

O Lord, You have called us to be a holy people. Too often we do not want to be! Please forgive us and remind us again.

Did book signing at downtown Borders in Indianapolis. As usual, left my car in parking lot at Saint John's Catholic Church, across from RCA Dome. Really good personnel with whom to work. New District Governor of Rotary Tom Fisher bought copy of *More Fast Food for the Soul*. Layout of the store and people passing through to go elsewhere made for difficult signing. Many in a hurry with little time to converse.

While I am almost as active in retirement as under full-time appointment, the freedom to pick and choose is great!

Continue to teach me, Lord, that faith and works are one package. They belong together.

As a young pastor, never in my wildest dreams did I ever think I would do book signings in downtown Indianapolis!

SATURDAY, JULY 12TH

Life and death—death and life, O Lord. Please be gentle with us as we get older. Keep us continually fixed on our salvation.

Went to north side of Fort Wayne and did book signing at Family Christian Book Store. It was the first time there for me. The store was spacious, well-organized, and ideal for signing. I was situated in the wide center aisle near the front. Inspired by several young people, teens and beyond.

Gave thanks for cordial relationships with Roman Catholic priests in Muncie: Fathers Dennis Goth (Saint Lawrence), Ed Kacena (Saint Mary), John Kieffer (Saint Francis), and William Grady (Saint Mary—now deceased). This covers most of ten years.

Returned home and somewhat troubled by my wife's ongoing coughing. I need to stay reasonably close to help her.

O God, I pray for those marriages of man and wife that are in trouble. We have lost so much in marital faithfulness. In this area, our decadence must surely be stirring Your anger.

SUNDAY, JULY 13TH

There is a fountain filled with blood drawn from Emmanuel's veins. Sinners plunged beneath that flood lose all their guilty stains.

Where would we be without the precious and holy blood of our Savior, Jesus the Christ? Our spiritual life would be greatly diminished, perhaps even non-existent.

Went to worship alone and then later took my wife to our favorite restaurant, the Olive Garden. Good times!

So happy Jon Rye Kinghorn, an old college friend, and I have been able to share our lives in recent years.

O Lord, hold me tightly. I feel most comfortable that way! Grant all of us in our little family a safe journey throughout the night.

MONDAY, JULY 14TH

O Lord, teach us to accept our weaknesses and frailties, giving them humbly to you for correction. We belong to You, O Lord.

Wrote a reference for Mark L. Eutsler so he can enter the UMC lay ministry program. He is a remarkable man for his energy, versatility, and vast interests. He is an Associate.

Looked through some of deceased daughter Anne's papers and books. She was a very sensitive and spiritually oriented young woman. During her senior year in Seymour High School (Indiana), her Christmas gift to me was *Jesus Son of Man* by Rudolf Augstein. In her hand-written inscription she wrote, "To my Dad . . . if this book disillusions you, you can live with it so if life disillusions you (even to destroying your beliefs) you can live life and deal with it . . . Always, Anne."

So, mystery—sometimes with heartbreak—is a part of all our lives. Yet, in the midst of the storms there is always God, omnipresent and omnipotent.

The only satisfying way to live our lives is with an attitude of gratitude.

TUESDAY, JULY 15TH

Call us to be thankful, O Lord, for every moment of our lives on this earth. Then, we shall live forever where time is no longer a factor.

Continued working on my paper for the First International Congress (ESBVM-USA). Really, putting the finishing touches to it. Holy Spirit present.

So grateful for being able to coordinate three different ministries (pastoral, literary, and ecumenical) for much of my life. Despite some thinking, I always did the basics for all of my pastorates.

Reflected on my pastoral appointment to Argos (Indiana) UMC (1991–1993). The church has done very well in recent years and I expected it would. Roadblocks were managed and no longer became a factor.

Special persons there were: Joe and Anita Krom, Barry and Portia Wampler, Mary Ann Zentz, Helen Tucker, Hugh Umbaugh, Evelyn Beam, Gerald and Helen Hess, Otto Gates, and Mike Howton.

WEDNESDAY, JULY 16TH

Let us sing in tune with Your holy angels, O Lord. Grant it would be moments of blessed harmony.

Needed to attend long Rotary meeting in New Castle because of district governor's visit. Hopefully, this will be my last long meeting for the club!

Moments of reflecting on my health and the wonderful days I have had. If something serious comes, trusting the dear Lord will warn me.

Dorothy and I took the evening off and went to Mounds Mall in Anderson. We ate at MCL and shopped for a time.

As usual, took late evening walk in subdivision for half hour or so. It is important I walk alone, undisturbed.

THURSDAY, JULY 17TH

Heal us, O Lord, especially among the clergy of all facets of the Christian Faith. Too often we are alienated and divided among ourselves.

Left soon after breakfast to go to Franklin United Methodist Home (Indiana), a retirement home for more than six hundred residents. Several visited and a few purchased books. Among retired ministers coming by were: Dick Christopher, Bob Fair, and Bill Offut. Joe Trueblood, administrator, was kind and friendly. Much appreciated Kathryn Koenig's visit; she is the widow of Bob Koenig, pastor and ecumenist.

Probably the greatest discomfort and disorientation I found in pastoring was two parishes where spiritual depth appeared to be virtually non-existent: Princeton First (now Hillside) and Rushville Saint Paul. Both turned out to be brief appointments. I may have expected too much too quickly in this matter. However, churches must always be more than secular places, where our Lord is seldom—if ever—at the center of people's lives.

Yes, Lord, heal us in the churches. Grant Your Holy Spirit would reign supreme and the clergy would be in tune!

We are called to give thanks for every opportunity placed in our midst, today and tomorrow—yes, now and forever.

FRIDAY, JULY 18TH

Your grace, O Lord. Save us from becoming so wayward that our planet becomes a holocaust. We beg of You that Your grace continues unabated among us.

Did essential correspondence, especially letters of gratitude to appropriate persons. Trusting that the Holy Spirit goes with my words and pervades them.

Sent birthday cards and checks to Donna (Lacy) and Terry Beyl, which is my usual manner of recognizing our little family. Both are really kind to us and generous in different ways. We have experienced this many times over the years and are truly grateful. Their professional successes are there for all to see. Their care of son Fillip is encompassing and some days for Grandfather Lacy truly remarkable!

How blessed I am to have those in our little family who genuinely care for one another. For this, my gratitude runs to overflowing.

The past, present, and future are all linked. While the past is the past, we do become what we have been becoming!

SATURDAY, JULY 19TH

Keep us ever safe, O Lord, from the snares of this life. Help us always to rest in the assurance of your presence.

Went to Walden's in Greenwood Mall to do a book signing. Aaron and I have worked together at least three other times. He is very supportive. Slow flow of traffic in the mall. Eventually, the signing went well and I was delighted. I always pray! In ministry, the results are invariably in God's hands and often we don't know what they are for years to come.

Lord, please be especially with Dorothy. Her pressures of family relationships and wanting to do more than she is able to do make for more and more stress.

Thank You, Lord, for all of Your care and concern. Please protect my good name and all that goes with it.

Father, Son, and Holy Spirit are eternal persons who are separate and distinct and yet completely harmonious in the ongoing life of the Trinity.

SUNDAY, JULY 20TH

Let us celebrate our Christian lives and give thanks for Jesus the Christ! He is our Savior and Lord, now and forevermore.

Went to Corinth UMC, near Muncie, to preach twice—once at 9:00 AM and the other at 11:00 AM. Met by Gary Kirkham, lay leader. The first was traditional and the second contemporary. Second was especially well-attended with many young people. Excellent lay leadership in both services.

Truly grateful for Ray Waddle's feature story in *Interpreter* magazine published in July-August issue of 2003. He interviewed me and ran a picture. The feature in its entirety focused on ecumenism. He ran my "Decalogue for Ecumenical Discipleship," which has been influential for several years. Copies of the magazine went to all United Methodist churches in the USA.

While denominational loyalties make for cohesion, they can also perpetuate a kind of suffocating allegiance and rob us of a much bigger, better picture.

Dear God, give Your people holiness that separates us from the world and yet enables us to witness for Christ and His Church.

MONDAY, JULY 21ST

Keep me ever humble, O Lord, and in harmony with Your Holy Spirit. Use me as You see fit for the upbuilding of Your Kingdom.

Did my monthly Associates newsletter and was able to mail it in the afternoon. The number has slipped to fewer than thirty.

Called the Archdiocese of Indianapolis for their ecumenical officer. They don't have one! For years, Father Thomas Murphy handled that and we worked together with successes.

The ecumenical enterprise seems more and more confusing, even mysterious. As long as the Holy Spirit is leading, that's just fine!

I give thanks, O Lord, for what has been, what is, and what shall be. Please keep my loved ones in Your care at all times.

TUESDAY, JULY 22ND

The Father's love has no limits, as evidenced in the crucifixion and resurrection of His only Son, Jesus the Christ.

A mostly relaxing day, catching up with correspondence and contacting book stores. New signings were scheduled.

Received our daughter (Donna), son-in-law (Terry), and grandson (Fillip) for her birthday dinner. Lovely meal, special sharing. She is forty-five. Born in Kokomo during my pastorate at Trinity UMC there.

Fillip is spending the night and will go on a trip with us tomorrow. We hope to surprise him. His parents see that he has many important opportunities.

Sometimes wished I had kept better records with detailed accounts of my funerals. I do know there were well more than four hundred. I considered all of them significant and attempted to minister carefully to all concerned.

WEDNESDAY, JULY 23RD

Call us, O Lord, into a deeper and more profound relationship with You. Cause us to be like children, willing to be taught.

Left at 7:00 AM for Shipshewana, Indiana for a festive day with the Amish and the enormous flea market. Fillip, Dorothy, and I made the trip and were delighted with the day of unique shopping, food, and explorations. Returned via Warsaw, Indiana and ate at Richards Restaurant.

Lord, sometimes we just need a change of pace! So often I have either not felt welcome during such ventures or had matters of ministry needing to be done. The trip felt good.

When I was Fillip's age, I was adjusting to going from Blountsville, Indiana school system to the Center system, a township school in Delaware County, Indiana. By today's standards, both were very small in numbers.

At times, O Lord, I believe the reciting of our creeds get in the way of practicing the Christian life.

THURSDAY, JULY 24TH

The Holy Bible, O Lord, is Your word to us. Keep it ever at the top of our reading lists to be prayerfully absorbed.

Sent advance copies of my manuscript for the ESBVM Congress to Robert King of the *The Indianapolis Star* and Dan Gangler (UMC Indiana Area Communications).

Visited with old friend Dave Wilson of Indianapolis Archdiocese. He is a very valuable layman for Roman Catholics.

Took Dorothy and Fillip to historic Farmland, Indiana. We had plenty of ice cream! It was a fun time for all of us.

As Fillip was taken back to his home in Fishers by his parents, we bid him goodbye. We also celebrated our two days with him.

FRIDAY, JULY 25TH

Reveal in me, O Lord, all of the truth You have for me. Cause me to deliberate in full harmony with Your Holy Spirit.

Areas of my soul that need further uprooting and purifying are Yours, O Lord. Do with them what You will.

Went to Barnes and Noble in Plainfield, Indiana to do a book signing. It was lengthy but in many ways successful.

I will touch every life You want me to touch, dear Lord, and no more or less. Grant Your will be done in my life and Your ways prevail.

Returned near midnight from signing and gave thanks to God for safe and accident-free driving. It seems the devil is always lurking!

SATURDAY, JULY 26TH

Keep reminding us, O Lord, all we can truly leave in this world is a genuinely good name that stands on its own.

Went to Family Christian Book Store on the east side of Indianapolis to do a book signing. Met lady from Richmond, Indiana who was related to some parishioner my father, Charles, had at Antioch Christian Church in Losantville, Indiana. He had been pastor there more than fifty years ago!

I have discovered book signings to be a remarkably unique way of doing ministry and certainly valid.

Once in a while I miss preaching every Sunday. Surprisingly, at the beginning of retirement, I never thought I could survive not preaching each Lord's day!

It is a gift to be able to meet and, to some extent, know thousands of people as a pastor/author/ecumenist.

SUNDAY, JULY 27TH

To God be the glory, great things He hath done! O come to the Father through Jesus, the Son. Praise the Lord! Let the people rejoice!

Worshipped at Saint Andrew Presbyterian. Worshipping outside of United Methodist churches, I continually find valuable and beneficial.

We enjoyed eating at Texas Roadhouse. Returned home and relaxed. Christie (Luellen) Fouse called and gave me a missionary's address—Danny Lacy (distant relative).

Reflected on my two eventful and growing years (1985–1987) at Salem Community UMC near Hebron, Indiana. Celebrated Holy Communion with real wine every Sunday!

Special laity that attended were Dean and Maxine Snider, Jim and Marian Hooseline, John Morland, Ray Searle, Jim Saqui, Dick Palmer, and Doris Shinaberger.

MONDAY, JULY 28TH

Dear Lord, the Holy Scriptures tell us to love one another, especially in the household of Faith. We beg of You, give us that gift.

Ate breakfast in local restaurant with my brother Mike. We enjoyed our time together and mostly talked about the past.

Visited by phone with the associate pastor at Losantville Antioch Christian Church (Indiana). Determined my father, Charles William Lacy, served there as pastor from 1954 to 1959. It was affiliated with the Congregational-Christian denomination and never joined the merger with the United Church of Christ. This was virtually a full-time ministry as opposed to some small part-time churches he served from time to time. It was and is a strong town church. I shall always remember his genuine Christian spirit and life.

As a little boy, I can remember my father smoking cigarettes. Then, he was converted and gave them up.

The revivalistic environment in east central Indiana that I experienced as a boy and youth has always carried with it both good news and bad news. For the most part, I never doubted the sincerity but was convinced lack of information and misinformation produced faulty spiritual vision.

TUESDAY, JULY 29TH

For Your love and unbounded mercy, O Lord, I give thanks. Keep me ever humble and obedient to Your Holy Spirit.

Visited the Anderson, Indiana Rotary Club as a makeup. Had been guest speaker for the club several months before that. Warmly greeted.

Like funerals, wished I had better records for the weddings at which I officiated. There were, at least, four hundred. I always liked to observe the face of the bride. It seemed to tell a great deal about the future!

Hope and pray those getting married accepted the ceremony as sacramental and for a lifetime. I worked very hard in that direction at the counseling sessions.

Surveyed my ministry for the near future. Obviously, the dear Lord is not through with me. Trust and obey . . . there is no other way.

WEDNESDAY, JULY 30TH

Give us Your wisdom, O Lord, and teach us to live by it. Deep down we know what really matters most is the daily living that manifests Christ.

Attended New Castle Rotary meeting. Guest speaker was Howard Caldwell, an icon in broadcasting across central Indiana. I visited briefly with Howard afterward. He freely shared his mind about his pastors: first, E. Carver McGriff, and second, M. Kent Millard (Saint Luke's UMC, Indianapolis).

Discovered in the media that Tim Durham had built an upscale restaurant in downtown New Castle. Widely known for his wealth and lifestyle, he and his family were in my church in Seymour (1974–1979).

Recalled my first funeral was for Spiceland UMC, just south of New Castle. I was twenty-four and she was ninety-six, so the deceased was four times my age! This was in 1957. I was still teaching school in Dunkirk at the time.

Love knows no bounds and that's hard for us to learn, Lord, because all of us can be so unlovely!

THURSDAY, JULY 31ST

How little we are, O God, how little we are! Yet, You care about us in ways we know and mostly do not know about.

O God, what is more thrilling and satisfying than to be a part of Your Kingdom? Yes, everything and everyone matter. Yet, nothing else and no one else matter!

Reflected upon the numerous worthwhile activities and meetings in the service clubs and other organizations of which I have been a part.

Gave thanks for two very talented clergymen with whom I served as a colleague during my First UMC Hagerstown years (1966–1970). They were John U. Miller and George Kuebler. John was a tremendous orator and George had excellent expertise in counseling. They were at the UCC church, hardly two blocks away. It was a congregation with several Perfect Circle and Dana executives.

My predecessor in Hagerstown was James Powell and my successor was Harry Hashberger. Theologically, they were quite different, but I believe sincere.

AUGUST
2 0 0 8

FRIDAY, AUGUST 1ST

Thank You, Lord, for the nudges of Your Holy Spirit. Recently, they have been more clear to me. I beg of You that this will continue.

Went to Family Christian Book Store in Carmel for signing. It was a time of ministry over and above signing books. It's so marvelous and in a way mysterious, O God, the opportunities You lay before us. We really cannot plan them and mostly cannot predict them. One lovely young family bought three of my books and visited with me at length; the husband was a special blessing. During the signings, Grace Community Church in Noblesville, Indiana was mentioned a few times. Apparently, it has grown into a huge church.

As I look into the future, how shall I ever live long enough to make use of the countless opportunities given by a loving and just God?

Reminisced about my long walks during my days as a college student in Muncie. A couple miles for a simple cup of coffee was profoundly therapeutic!

Our days are numbered on this earth and yet they are ours; we can mostly do with them what we choose.

SATURDAY, AUGUST 2ND

Purify my heart and mind, O God. Make them so they can react within Your will to the slightest wooing of the Holy Spirit.

The book signing at Borders in Carmel was a gem. Eighteen copies were sold with little effort. My soul felt so good!

While much planning and implementation goes into these signings, often it is the people I meet coming and going that inspire me. Take the young mother, who sat alone in an MCL restaurant in Carmel with her two little girls under school age. She held their hands and prayed openly. I shook hands with her and complimented her, plus giving her two complimentary copies of my books. She smiled and her eyes glistened with tears.

Sometimes we need to pray for those who live near us but seldom see. Farmington Meadows (Muncie), where I live, is a good place to do that.

Once in awhile I attempt to understand the lives of my parents better. That is one big order and I am not sure I do it very well!

SUNDAY, AUGUST 3RD

O Father, thank You for this life and its numerous blessings. I look forward to heaven and all that will bring.

Worshipped at Muncie High Street UMC. Holy Communion was celebrated and I was able to kneel at the railing with others. Praise God!

Reflected on my high school years (1946–1950) at Center in Perry Township of Delaware County, Indiana. Ongoing friends not in my graduating class and mostly older are remembered with appreciation. Among them were: Wendell Keesling, Wayne Leedy, Bud Conwell, Rita Affert, Loretta Harris, Jack Hatcher, Sterl Huber, George Harris, Margaret Hamilton, Don Black, Les Schull, Suzanne Koontz, Dorothy Perry, and Joe Duncan.

As most know, after graduating from high school, life is never the same. Most go their own ways and only occasionally, perhaps never, see one another again. A permanent, well-run alumni association sometimes is able to bridge the gap.

The heat of the summer is a great time to slow down and vacation. I like all of the seasons with the distinctiveness each brings.

MONDAY, AUGUST 4TH

Thank You, dear Lord, for giving me such a wonderful little family. I only wish Anne Marie could be physically among us.

In spite of our meanderings and belligerence, You are with us. Sometimes we have to be saved from ourselves!

My former congregations and constituents are always dear to me. Please, Father, tell all of them I care about them and affirm their current pastors.

The cloud of witnesses is always there and some day I will get to meet them. Their faithful prayers and watchfulness give me strength.

Please take good care of my Dorothy. Her health is so very fragile. Thank You for her courage and her commitment. You gave her to me so long ago.

TUESDAY, AUGUST 5TH

O God, Your timing is always right and we invariably seem reluctant to admit it. Keep us ever humble and give us Your gift of righteousness.

Helpful phone calls made to friends on the book signing circuit. Some have been so helpful and I am grateful!

Did shopping at J.C. Penney in Muncie Mall. My daughters Donna and Martha have been very good to give me gift cards. I love them and appreciate them.

Spoke to the Evening Lions Club in Anderson. Mixture of people who had known failure first-hand and were struggling. Treated with respect, but not sure how well I was received.

I was president of the Lions Club for a year during my Hagerstown pastorate (1966–1970). Fellow Lions made me look good! Paul R. Foulke was a key member of both the club and UMC.

WEDNESDAY, AUGUST 6TH

All things come from Thee, O God. You are the Creator and we are Your created.

Rotary meeting was at the Art Center in New Castle. Excellent presentation by Kim Galyen, wife of Henry County Public Defender Jeff Galyen.

Conducted personal business in both New Castle and Muncie. The UMC Board of Pension has been good to us!

Spoke at length by phone with Steve Cherry, pastor of First UMC in Seymour, Indiana. I was pastor there from 1974 to 1979. For years it was known as the church with many power brokers. Apparently, that is no longer true.

Holy Spirit, guide us in all our pathways. Keep us sensitive to the way we would ideally like things and the way they really are.

THURSDAY, AUGUST 7TH

Your loving care, O God, gives us more than all the world can provide with its promises and allurements.

Time to do desktop sifting and sorting, followed by tossing used and outdated materials into the waste basket.

Martha arrived with Justin Daniel somewhat before noon. We immensely enjoyed our time with them.

So grateful for Martha's marriage to Jeff, who is a native of North Dakota. Natalie Rene was at the Goddard, a private school, for the day.

God answers prayers in His ways. She, Jeff, and their children make for a joyful and lovable foursome. I give thanks!

FRIDAY, AUGUST 8TH

Strengthen Your servant, O Lord. Give him the endurance necessary for living these days in a victorious fashion.

Worked on column for *The Star Press* (Muncie). It is taking more time than normal. As usual, trying to build bridges!

Dorothy and I shopped in the new Hamilton Town Center, just off Interstate 69. The weather was pleasant and good for walking. Met old friend Dan Motto at Borders. His pastoral heart was grieving over a difficult situation in one of his churches.

Went to Fillip's Tae Kwon Do meeting in Indianapolis. He was impressive and attained a higher belt.

Yes, the Lord does give and take away. Eventually, everyone and everything do His will.

SATURDAY, AUGUST 9TH

Strengthen me, O Lord, for I am weak. My weakness translates into cowardice and procrastination. Your grace, O Lord!

Went to Lafayette for book signing at Barnes and Noble. Sales were marginal and store manager did not seem to want me around.

Drive home was in a rainstorm. Gave thanks to God for His presence and care. He rides with me!

When we sense injustice, it is hard not to become angry. Help me, Lord, to be Your disciple . . . when I am joyful or sorrowful.

I give thanks for my life and for the way I was treated by my father and mother, plus my grandparents.

SUNDAY, AUGUST 10TH

Quiet my fears, dear Lord, and grant me Your holy confidence. I am one of Your sons, who needs a sign of Your faithfulness.

We worshipped at New Burlington UMC, just southeast of Muncie, and were warmly greeted. Charles Kirklin and Phil Lawson are leading figures there. I knew their fathers and mothers. Matthew Leffler preached a quality sermon both homiletically and theologically. O Lord, I trust in You to inspire him and other young men in the ordained ministry.

Continue to appreciate old friends Bill Cross (Cokesbury), Stan Hicks (Berean Books), David E. Sumner (Ball State), and Gil Stafford (Church of God, Anderson).

We went to brother Mike's near Parker City, Indiana, to visit his son Brad and wife, Laura. They reside in Nevada and have two growing sons that are on their way to becoming men of honor. Good visit!

Can't help wondering about the preaching of hell-fire and brimstone. Generally, I strongly suspect we need more a sense of this part of the Gospel from the pulpit.

MONDAY, AUGUST 11TH

God of glory and God of love, I give thanks for Your blessings. Some are seen and many go unseen. Our prayers are in praise and gratitude.

Left just after 6:00 AM for Pittsburgh and the First International Congress-Ecumenical Society of the Blessed Virgin Mary USA. Hopeful!

Except for construction and delays in Pittsburgh proper, it was an easy drive. Arrived at Holiday Inn Pittsburgh-University Center about 2:30 PM.

Able to attend the Rev. Jennifer Matison Juliano's talk. She presented an exegesis on Revelation 12:13–17. She is pastor of First Congregational Church in Walton, New York.

Spent quiet evening in the motel and checking out the meeting areas for the congress. Struck by how crowded everything seemed to be!

TUESDAY, AUGUST 12TH

Awaken me, Lord, with prayers for the day. Call me to concentrate on the work at hand. Grant Your Holy spirit among us.

Listened to Maura Hearden's presentation dealing with reflections on the Marian dimension of Catholic-Methodist Dialogue. Well-prepared and presented. She had contacted me some months ago, seeking my help for the completion of her doctoral program. Maura is scheduled to be on the faculty at DeSales University in Center Valley, Pennsylvania.

Gave my presentation at the Newman Center. It emphasized Mary should be an imperative in worship, study, and witnessing among Protestants. Response was positive and I felt affirmed by the group. The fact I was the only United Methodist at this First International Congress was of interest to some!

Social interacting was valuable and especially gave a chance to spend some unhurried time with those we see once or twice each year.

O God, call us always to be charitable with one another in our ecumenical ministry.

WEDNESDAY, AUGUST 13TH

More opportunities! Thank You, Lord, for all of them and please keep me in harmony with the Holy Spirit.

Listened to Mary Catherine Nolan's presentation on Mary and Islam. While some disjointed, it was interesting and even somewhat intriguing. The Koran has more to say about Mary than Jesus!

Delighted to hear Father Peter Stravinskas speak and especially to meet him for the initial time! We have communicated for years and I have written for his publications, such as *The Catholic Answer, Our Sunday Visitor,* and *Catholic Response.* A brilliant man, Peter spoke on the Blessed Virgin according to the Reformers. He pointed out Luther, Calvin, and Zwingli were committed to Mariology.

Attended a lovely closing banquet at the motel for all registrants. Sat with Bruce Lawrence, a devout Orthodox. I gave the invocation prior to eating.

Began to reflect on the entire event and, frankly, was impressed. For one thing, ESBVM-USA moved out of a solely national group and became one with beginning international connections.

THURSDAY, AUGUST 14TH

Holy, holy, holy, early in the morning, our song shall rise to Thee. It has been a time of sharing with comrades and stimulating presentations.

Started home about 6:00 AM and easily, even surprisingly, found my way quickly out of Pittsburgh. Motored several miles before eating at a Bob Evans.

Reflected along the way about Bill Ryon (Virginia), Virginia Kimball (Massachusetts), and Judith Gentle (Pennsylvania). Their commitment and leadership made this extraordinary event possible. So, our First International Congress has occurred.

Arrived in late afternoon, ahead of Dorothy's return trip from Indianapolis. Glad to greet her and sense her health was not a problem.

Mail from the four days was at a minimum. Phone calls and e-mails were also light. That made for some pleasant conversation between husband and wife.

FRIDAY, AUGUST 15TH

Days and nights come and go, Lord Jesus, but You remain ever near and I sense security. Thank You!

In mid-morning headed for Miamisburg, Ohio (suburban Dayton) and book signing for a Family Christian Book Store. Kevin, the store manager, greeted me warmly. Inspired by the congenial response of several people. Book sales above average. Since it was a new store for me, I was encouraged. Store manager invited me back near Christmas. It is a quick and easy trip of less than two hours. I will likely accept.

Returned home at a reasonable hour and in my own quiet way celebrated the trip and event. Some good people out there!

Sometimes I feel like "I'm on the road again" every other day or so. Events are mostly fulfilling and something I could definitely not do in full-time appointment.

Christians need to celebrate more, not because they have acquired an affluent lifestyle and suffered less than others, but because the Holy Spirit abides, provides, and guides.

SATURDAY, AUGUST 16TH

Busy times, Lord. Hold me steady and supply the needed direction. I always cherish Your protection and give thanks for it.

Left for Florence, Kentucky (suburban Cincinnati) to book signing in the Barnes and Noble. Manager, Joan, well-prepared. I had been there one other time. Great day for signing. Excellent flow of traffic and many interested folks. Sold thirty copies and probably could have sold more.

Stopped at a Perkins restaurant on Interstate 74 to eat. Delicious salmon dinner and waitress was respectful and capable.

All in all, truly a successful trip. Will likely return there. This Barnes and Noble store more small town and relational than most I have known.

There are many more authors of books in the religious field today than when I began in 1974 (*Gems from James*), which was my first published book. Actually, my first published article was in 1960, but my literary history is a story all unto itself.

SUNDAY, AUGUST 17TH

This is the day the Lord has made. Let us rejoice and be glad in it. Look forward to visiting churches and not having to preach!

Visited a Presbyterian church. Pastor had well-modulated voice and was well-prepared. Despite some thinking, professionalism in the pulpit is not all bad!

Dorothy and I enjoyed ourselves at Ruby Tuesday's. Excellent service and, as always, quality food. Overall, it is probably the best restaurant that we frequent.

Did taped interview with Kathryn Raaker. This was scheduled to run on five radio stations including one in Cincinnati. Appeared to be fruitful. I guess we shall see! Glad for the opportunity.

Retired for the night, giving thanks for this life and the hope of one much better to come. Thank You, Lord, for everything and everyone.

MONDAY, AUGUST 18TH

Through pain and sorrow, You are there, O Lord. During all times and all places, You are there, O Lord. Remind us!

A day of catching up. More than a week of necessary writing had piled up. But my memory was good and God inspired!

E-mails from Dan Gangler, area communications director for UMC, and others produced ongoing responses. Dan has now married a Jewish lady!

Father, You have blessed me with co-workers that I mostly admire and trust. Please send more colleagues to distribute my published materials.

Tomorrow is our daughter Sharon's birthday. She will be forty-four. She was born at Ball Memorial Hospital in Muncie.

TUESDAY, AUGUST 19TH

O Lamb of God, Who takes away the sins of the world, we beg of You to give America a new birth. Our sins are many and pervasive.

Went to very large gathering of clergy and laity in Greenwood, Indiana, at Byrd's Cafeteria for a noon meal. There were five hundred or so! Governor Mitch Daniels spoke and I was thoroughly inspired! For the first time, I learned he was an active member and office holder at Tabernacle Presbyterian Church in Indianapolis. His servant model of government ministry was an amazing word for us. I could hardly believe my ears!

While church and state are separate in our country, that does not mean they never touch one another for the good of all concerned.

My wife and I took Sharon out for her birthday at O'Charley's in Fishers. It was a cherished moment. Bless her heart!

As You bless our nation, Lord, remind us that in time You demand justice and no one is exempt.

WEDNESDAY, AUGUST 20TH

Unto You, O God, we owe all thanksgiving and praise. Keep us ever humble before Your almighty and everlasting throne.

Glad to be back in attendance at New Castle Rotary. Visited at length with the publisher, Tina West, of the local paper. Appreciated her strong religious orientation.

Also had even longer visit with Dave Burns, Presbyterian layman and past president of the club. He and his wife travel internationally. They are very interesting people.

Relaxed with sense of both accomplishment and fulfillment. That does not happen very often and perhaps it's a good thing it does not! Otherwise, we might rest on our laurels.

Dear Lord, help me always to remember our daughter Sharon in my daily prayers. She is deserving of recognition, respect, and love.

THURSDAY, AUGUST 21ST

O God, I celebrate this life—in particular—the wonderful little family You have given us. We cherish them and deeply love them.

Reflected on the busy weekend coming up in Cincinnati-area and Bloomington, Indiana. Hoping and praying for safe travels and the presence of the Holy Spirit.

Gave thanks for knowing Harvey Thornburg, long ago deceased, who was a Congregational-Christian minister in east central Indiana. He was a polished fellow, who had some brilliant things to say to me as a teenager.

Also, vividly remember Lester Sumrall (LESEA Network). I appeared on his television stations from time to time in South Bend, Indianapolis and beyond.

O Lord, keep me ever humble and attuned to the needs of people, near and far. Often I have not done well with a servant-type ministry that we are called to do.

FRIDAY, AUGUST 22ND

All things are in Your hands, O God. Help me to rest in the assurance You will never leave me nor forsake me.

Visited with a contact for Redkey (Indiana) Alumni Association. My first year of teaching was in that system (1954–1955). Taught five different classes and had a study hall in six periods! Those I remember best were the principal, Darrel Finch, and Dewitt Ogan, superintendent. Wilma Jean Addington was a favorite teaching colleague and I still communicate with her. I lived in the town that year and freely related to the people, including the First Methodist Church family.

The Shambargers were well known in Redkey: Tom and his son, John. John was an entertaining chef. After I was gone some years, their restaurant became nationally known through the *Wall Street Journal*. At one point in time, there were customer waiting lists of two years.

Remembered a parishioner, Herman Buckingham, at Leesburg UMC (1987–1990). He was an excellent sermon taster and would confer with me now and then. When I had his funeral, the family was very kind and grateful. He had a son who was a brigadier general.

Yes, Lord, keep us ever thankful for your many blessings that come through people.

SATURDAY, AUGUST 23RD

O Thou great Protector and Lover of my soul, I give thanks for Your ongoing mercies. Keep me ever humble before Your cross.

Left at 5:30 AM for Cincinnati and radio station WCVX for an interview on Kathryn Raaker's talk show. Very difficult finding the station suite in downtown Cincinnati. Finally, the dear Lord provided and I was there ready to go! A twenty minute interview went quite well. It seemed to flow with ease and she was careful to ask good questions.

Book signing at Barnes and Noble at Newport on the levee was good news/bad news. Excellent store promotion but too many rowdy youth.

Not really sold on becoming more of a national figure. Believe with my family and Dorothy's health, I am better off confining most events to the Midwest, specifically Indiana and Ohio.

Thought of Bob Stephens, basketball coach at Dunkirk High School during my time of teaching there. He and I were good friends. I helped him with the statistics for the games. Bob had an excellent record.

SUNDAY, AUGUST 24TH

O Creator, provider of all that has been, now is and ever shall be, I give thanks for the past, present, and future.

Left for Barnes and Noble in Bloomington to sign books and arrived on time. Drive from Nashville, Indiana to Bloomington is tricky but a beautiful one!

Not enough books arrived for a full signing and Michelle was very apologetic. She is a skilled coordinator and had no control over that. Event went well anyway and we used some of my inventory of books. There were excellent—even inspirational—conversations, especially from a retired RN.

Arrived home before 11:00 PM and was relieved. It had been a long day, but worthwhile with the Holy Spirit abiding.

Remind Christians, O Christ, of our continued duty to witness for You and Your Church. Faith without practice isn't much good.

MONDAY, AUGUST 25TH

Your loving mercy, O Lord, I truly want. Please supply all of my needs now and forevermore. Thank you.

Cared for necessary correspondence. Try to be always prompt in thanking those who are my colleagues and comrades, lay and clergy.

Received disturbing phone call from collection agency. Why don't such outfits do the necessary research, saving them time and others grief?

Our business and financial communities in this country have become often not only wasteful but more or less unethical. The Holy Spirit abides and provides for those trying to be ethical in difficult circumstances.

National Democratic Convention is underway. Democrats appear to be sorely divided. We shall see. Remember attending Indiana State Democratic Convention in Indianapolis soon after college graduation.

TUESDAY, AUGUST 26TH

Teach us, O Lord, to be fully dependent on You and Your Holy Spirit. We implore You to keep us ever in harmony with Your Holy Spirit.

It was a special day for us as grandparents. Martha came with her two delightful and precious children: Natalie Rene and Justin Daniel. Natalie is only three years of age and her maturity level is scary! Justin is nine months old and especially loves mommy!

Time passes and memorable events, such as these, come and go. Thank You, O Holy Christ, for each and every one of them.

Virginia Kimball, president of ESBVM-USA, and I spent an hour or so e-mailing each other. She is a Marian scholar of international reputation and a member of the Orthodox Church. She had several children and yet was able to earn a doctorate.

Tell us how to love one another, dear Lord. How much of it is our effort and how much is strictly a gift from You?

WEDNESDAY, AUGUST 27TH

Jesus the Christ, You are the Son of Man and the Son of God. My destiny belongs to You.

Went to Kokomo to speak to the Lions Club. We met at Martinos on the far north side in an impressive Italian restaurant. For a minute, I thought I might be in Chicago! Greeted warmly and my presentation was well-received. Frankly, it was an engaging time of congeniality and considerable interest. The group was composed of older men with several World War II veterans. It would appear the retirees were from managerial positions either from General Motors or Chrysler.

Took my wife to Sirloin Stockade for buffet. It was a refreshing time for us and she picked up gift cards for her fiftieth Center High School class party.

We would rather not carry Your cross, O Lord, but its benefits always exceed our expectation. It is the gateway to heaven!

O God, I have always cared about my family, but have never shown it very well. Help me to do better.

THURSDAY, AUGUST 28TH

Holy God, I need Your humility and self-discipline. In both areas, I am sometimes far too weak and powerless. Please provide.

Exhilarated by the spirit of the Democratic National Convention on television. Thrilled by the speeches and exuberance. The various divergent groups seeking unity was intriguing.

My early goal in high school was to be the governor of the state of Indiana. I would get there by first being an attorney or professor of American history. God took me a different route and I have been faithful and obedient to that calling. Yet, at the age of seventy-five, I still at times have ambitions for a political career!

Went to a special program with Dorothy at Ball Memorial Hospital in Muncie. Kurt Alexander was the speaker and he was excellent.

Could the USA become a theocratic state? Some historians say it was that during the Puritan era in New England.

FRIDAY, AUGUST 29TH

Ask God in sincerity and humility to immerse you in His grace and He will . . . on His terms!

Went to Muncie Sunrise Rotary Club for make-up. Sat with Don Black, retired school administrator. We were in high school together. He was a grade behind me and graduated in 1951. Our mothers were friends and our fathers were skilled in the plastering trade.

Headed to Richmond to do a book signing at Trinity Books and Gifts. Marcie, the manager, was very supportive. The event went well with several people coming from western Ohio.

Learned John McCain had named his vice presidential nominee, a young woman from Alaska: Governor Sarah Palin. Wow! As a committed wife and mother, she provides an inspirational model for public life. Believe her time will come in 2012 or 2016. Her greatest need is experience.

Arrived home safe and sound. Gave thanks to the living God for his goodness and protection.

SATURDAY, AUGUST 30TH

I cling to You, Lord, and trust in Your guidance with gratitude. Surely You are the hope of all humankind. Please dwell among us!

Reflected on the lives God has allowed me to touch. O Lord, so many were not in my churches! Sometimes I see that vast number of grains of sand on a beach.

The Catholic Moment, official newspaper of the Diocese of Lafayette in Indiana, made reference to my major gift on behalf of potential priests. Perhaps another gift of the Holy Spirit.

Even though the Chicago Cubs are in first place in their division, I watched the Philadelphia Phillies beat them this evening. I have followed the Cubs almost as far back as I can remember.

Yes, Lord, it is an attitude of gratitude—born of a right relationship with the Father through You—that we must always seek to have and apply. It seems so simple and yet so difficult!

SUNDAY, AUGUST 31ST

Glory be to the Father, the Son, and the Holy Spirit. As it was in the beginning, is now, and evermore shall be.

My wife and I took a full day away from Muncie. We worshipped at Fishers UMC and ate in a lovely restaurant. We wanted to see a movie but could not find anything that interested us, so we went shopping. It was a happy time.

Dorothy's father, Herman Thomas, was killed on his way to work in an automobile accident; she was only eight years old at the time. Her mother, Alice (Minske), never remarried. In addition to Dorothy, she reared two sons and another daughter. Alice was a courageous woman by most any standard. I have always admired her for her dedication. She passed away in her early fifties, now well over thirty years ago.

Always, Lord, prod us genuinely to care for people and give of ourselves as time and energy allow.

Only God has the books on everything and everyone! We are called to be His people, regardless of circumstances.

SEPTEMBER
2 0 0 8

MONDAY, SEPTEMBER 1ST

O Lord, teach me to be a more tolerant person and yet never to sacrifice the heart of our precious Faith.

A morning filled with reading and corresponding. Read some especially fine recent articles on preaching.

Found the Internet to be a major component for my literary and ecumenical outreach. So glad I learned how to use it!

Reflected on my brief appointment to Battleground UMC (1990–1991), near Lafayette. I was appointed there largely so another pastor had a place to go. It didn't work well for much of anybody! Nevertheless, I remember with affection Lloyd and Lillian Killion, Dale Christopher, Jo Holmes, Bob and Maxine Young, John and Patty Garrott, and Stacy and Betty Prough. I adored the battlefield near the church, where William Henry Harrison won the Battle of Tippecanoe in 1811, and spent time walking the area; I found it inspiring.

Life is a gift and wherever we are and with whomever we find ourselves; yes, and regardless of the circumstances, opportunity for enrichment is there.

TUESDAY, SEPTEMBER 2ND

Hail Mary, full of grace, the Lord is with you. How powerfully sweet it is to hear these words!

Believe the best term paper out of the many I did during my MDIV work (1958–1961) at Christian Theological Seminary was, "A Dialogue Between a Psychologist and a Theologian." The psychologist was Harry Stack Sullivan and the theologian was Donald Charles Lacy. It was one of the most creative things I have ever done.

Give thanks day in and day out for the many blessings God gives, often in disguise and hidden.

To name names is always to run the risk of omitting someone significant in your life but not to name anyone is a tragedy!

Dear Lord, I trust You will keep my little family from harm and protect each and everyone of us. I have now had a rather long life, Lord, but You keep calling on me. Thank you!

WEDNESDAY, SEPTEMBER 3RD

Your timing is always perfect, Lord. Too often I have gone about doing things in ways I considered timely. Thank You for Your patience.

An emotional, surprising, and learning episode continues to come back to me from time to time. It happened during my pastorate at Seymour First UMC (1974–1979). One Monday morning, a pastor friend, Dennis Brayman (UCC), came into my office and began to weep. I thought a close family member had passed away. It never occurred to me his pet dog had died and he was broken-hearted!

The National Republican Convention rolls on and the oratory is a delight. Most eyes seem to be fixed on Sarah Palin, vice presidential nominee and her family. If the Republicans win and John McCain dies in office, is she experienced enough to be president? As much as I like and respect her, my answer is "No."

I give myself to You, O Lord, for whatever part I may play in this momentous election. Grant Your will be done and Your ways prevail.

O God, our sins as a nation seem as many as the sands on the beaches across the world. Judgment will come but fortunately for us it is not the last word.

THURSDAY, SEPTEMBER 4TH

The Apostle Peter reminds us not to be afraid of anyone and not to worry. How wonderfully helpful those words are!

Recalled my six aunts, their husbands (uncles) and first cousins in the Lacy family. Mary Elizabeth (Joseph H. Stonebraker)—Harold Junior, Darrel Wayne, Larry Lee, and Jacqueline Kay; Erma Ella (F. Hopkins

Kleihauer)—Carole Lacy, Christian F. II, and F. Hopkins Junior; Arletta Marie (Howard Jester)—Virginia Ann, Byron Eugene, Phillip Dwayne, and Linda Marie; Marjorie Louise (Myron Luellen)—Christie Ruth; Patty Lou (Charles Keesling)—Catherine Marie and Gary Truitt; and Judith Ann (George Harter)—Daniel Joel, Donald Lee, and Timothy Joe.

All first cousins are younger than I am. However, Mary's three sons are near my age. Two aunts are younger than I am: Patty Lou and Judith Ann.

One uncle, Delma Vernon, died at the age of ten and I never knew him. He and my father were the only sons in the family.

Three of my uncles served in the Second World War (Stonebraker, Kleihauer, and Luellen).

FRIDAY, SEPTEMBER 5TH

Not only the present, but the future is in Your hands, Lord. Make of us what You will for the eternal good of all.

In the storms of this life, O Lord, only You can come and quiet us. Hopefully, we have fully learned this!

A big day for Dorothy. The fiftieth anniversary celebration of her graduating from Center High School (now Wapahani) is at hand. It was a festive occasion for those members and friends. She distributed her excellent pictorial and biographical directories she had meticulously done for them. I sat by her side and observed the group. It was quite a learning experience. I was so happy for her.

Life, in many ways, remains a mystery, but there is the assurance the heavenly Father cares about us.

Our good deeds do not go unnoticed, but grant, O God, we never do them just to be seen and thanked!

SATURDAY, SEPTEMBER 6TH

Grant Your grace, dear God, to this sometimes weary seventy-five-year-old man. He wants to do right and to be right in all his coming and going.

Some of us in the clergy seem so spoiled. We take too much for granted. Our eyes too often do not seriously look into the heavens. Our sins are many and sadly some of them seem to be so respectable!

Went to the Center High School Alumni banquet for all classes. Not as many this year as last, but a good crowd of one hundred fifty or so. Dorothy's class was now honored before the entire group. She was given praise and some monetary gifts. I enjoyed myself and sat near my class of 1950. Other classmates that were there were Anita Oxley, Bonnie Warner, and Betty Warner. Bonnie and Betty are twins.

Every life is so precious, Lord, and to think there are those who would never allow birth to occur!

Our lives seem so brief and yet they are given to us for ministry in whatever form that takes.

SUNDAY, SEPTEMBER 7TH

Thank You, O Lord, for your goodness to me. I know it is unmerited. There is nothing I could do or refrain from doing that would make me worthy of Your goodness.

Reflected on the Walradth family of aunts, uncles, and first cousins. Glendabell (Ray Mitchell)—Patricia and David; Berl Eli (Joan Miller)—Deborah, Randall, and Greg; and Verl Isaac (Marjorie Everett)—Lynn and Larry. Robert Wayne had three children by Dorothy (Williams)—Diana Lynn, Robert W. II, and Rita Kay. He also had three children by Christine (Johnson)—Cheryl Ann, Charles Eric, and Donna Marie. For some years now, he has been married to Barbara Lee (Stephens).

I am the oldest of the first cousins. In fact, I could easily be a father to most of them. My thirty years out of east central Indiana has caused me either to re-acquaint or acquaint myself.

Family relationships can be so complicated and yet so simple in some ways we tend to disregard significant happenings.

One of the most insightful and valuable books I ever read dealt with healing the family tree. The Sacrament of Holy Communion is a means to bring this about.

MONDAY, SEPTEMBER 8TH

Bring to our hearts and minds, Father, to tell others we love them and to keep on telling them we love them by word and deed, until they believe it.

Left early for Plymouth, Indiana to attend a Christian Unity Committee meeting. We met at our favorite place, Bob Evans. Only three of us were in attendance: John Gosser, Ron Liechty, and myself. Formalities were dropped and it was a time of ecumenical and personal sharing, sometimes with a bit of argumentation!

Returned home and bought birthday cards for son-in-law Jeffrey John Graham and grandson Fillip A. L. Beyl.

When the tension and anxiety subside, how good it is, O Lord! To relax in the arms of a loving and protective God is simply awesome.

How much power does God delegate to us? I will never know the answer to that one in this life!

TUESDAY, SEPTEMBER 9TH

All thanks be to You, O Lord, who loves far beyond our comprehensions. Only in Your presence is life worth living.

Today is our oldest daughter's birthday. If Anne Marie were living, she would be forty-eight years of age. Her tragic death at the age of thirty-five causes me pain and sorrow almost daily. Nevertheless, a loving God understands and causes me to pray everyday for her. She is still one of my girls for whom I deeply care. So, we shall meet again in eternity. We shall rest in Your holy and provident care, O God. Let the angels sing in victory and the universal soul of her Catholic Faith sustain her.

Recalled the several different Bibles I have used over these many years. We have been blessed by the quality of them.

Most of my life I have been a voracious reader. The thrill of the ideas stated still is much with me, but in a different sense. I must be more independent of those who have shared their wisdom.

The most potent of all things that can destroy a marriage is for one to be unfaithful and the other seek revenge by doing the same thing. In all my years of pastoring, I have never seen a marriage survive a double betrayal.

WEDNESDAY, SEPTEMBER 10TH

Your priceless salvation, O God, gives me great joy and boundless hope! To be a sinner saved by your grace is a wonder to behold.

Went to New Castle early and enjoyed Bob Evans coffee. *USA Today* added to my sense of beginning the day aright!

The Rotary program was by a man who had made a recent trip to Israel. Appreciated his candor and infectious personality. Such truly good ministry happens beyond so-called religious structures. I consider this a great blessing!

Many television stations continue to present aggressively the ongoing political and sometimes religious controversies, usually connected to the nominations at the national level.

We are to be inspired daily to spread the gratitude due to Almighty God and others. There is so much we don't know and yet there is a great deal we do know, one of which is the imperative nature of gratitude in order to live abundantly.

THURSDAY, SEPTEMBER 11TH

The Twin Towers in New York City came down by the hands of terrorists seven years ago. O God, we were put on alert! Help us never to forget.

It is Jeff Graham my son-in-law's birthday. I find him a solid husband and loving father. My prayers of long ago were answered. Thank You, Jesus.

Wrote column for *The Star Press* that focused on Sarah Palin. O God, grant Your will be done in her life and Your ways prevail.

Reflected on pastorate at Saint James East UMC (1973–1974) in Evansville, now McCutchanville Community UMC. They were former EUB's and I was their first Methodist pastor. Dear and faithful people there were Josette Higgins, Irvin Griepenstroh, Gary Schaar, Charles Picket, Charles Goldman, Winona Royer, David Dixon, and Rudy Hufnagel.

While the United Methodist system of appointing pastors to churches has its critics, I do hope the stability and security inherent in such polity continues.

FRIDAY, SEPTEMBER 12TH

Jesus calls us to follow Him daily throughout this world. He calls eternally important but wayward human beings to follow Him. Do you hear Him?

Went to Walden's in Terre Haute to do book signing. A safe and pleasant trip through heavy traffic. Many positive conversations at the event. There was special interest shown in my *Collected Works*, which surprised me. The support and cooperation of the staff made it an inspiration. The Holy Spirit sent me helpers and I give thanks!

Arrived home with heavy tension from driving. Took time to unwind and reflect on the many positive comments about my work.

Successes come and go. After all, what is success or failure for that matter? In the long run all of this is most assuredly God's business.

Terre Haute bookstores have been fruitful for me. The intersection of Interstate 70 and Highway 41 makes for many shoppers and religious folks looking for good books!

SATURDAY, SEPTEMBER 13TH

Invite us to Your deeper dimensions for our sake, O Lord, and with Your help we shall grow in the Faith.

Went to Barnes and Noble in Dayton to do book signing. It went well and the conversations were stimulating. Much spiritual hunger today!

Gave thanks for safe trip home. I love Your Kingdom, Lord, and earnestly desire forever to be a part of it.

Pondered the amazing life I have had. God has not only been good; He has blessed me with countless opportunities.

Look forward to grandson Fillip's birthday party tomorrow. He will be twelve years old and I am presenting him with his first Bible.

SUNDAY, SEPTEMBER 14TH

Teach us, O God, about Your old/new real presence in the Holy Communion. Indeed, You have not left us merely symbol and memorial!

Went to worship at First UMC Hagerstown to hear Kevin Giggy guest preach. When I was pastor there (1966–1970), he was just a boy. His sermon was spirited and well-planned. He told the congregation I made him nervous, which was a compliment I had not counted on!

My wife and I then headed for grandson Fillip's birthday party in Fishers. His birth date is really September 17th. His gifts were many and, in some cases, quite expensive. The Bible I gave him was carefully inscribed on the inside.

Have grown to love social and celebrative events of our little family. The Holy Spirit is at work in all of us and that shows!

At the end of the day I felt a sense of fulfillment and satisfaction. God is to be thanked.

MONDAY, SEPTEMBER 15TH

He leads me by still waters and restores my soul. Only You, dear Lord, can do that for us. Thank You!

Giving thanks for my doctor of ministry program at CTS from 1974 to 1976 and especially the key laity at Seymour First UMC, who directly participated in my doctoral project. It was entitled "Preaching as a Lay/Clergy Event." They were: Luella Abell, Thelma Lisman, Ed Pollen, Valerie Scott, Lloyd Kerkhof, Tom Johnson, Jim Aker, and Herb Jenkinson. They attended sessions with the text and a skeletal outline before them and asked to make comments each week prior to preaching the sermon. I took all comments into consideration before writing the sermon. This consumed nine consecutive weeks. They then listened to and read the sermons for the project and compared them to others in which they had no input on the basis of understanding, focus, continuity, relevance, sincerity, truth, and practicality. The compilation of their grading indicated they were happier with the ones in which they had input! I believe this is the kind of thing all pastors should do from time to time. It keeps us in touch with the living concerns of the congregation.

The city of Seymour has become a major hub of business at the intersection of Interstate 65 and Highway 50 in the center of southern Indiana.

Geographically, my appointments covered much of Indiana. I found this to be very rewarding.

I had wanted a doctorate from the time I left college and even before. The DMIN was primarily a professional degree, but I handled it in such a way it became strongly academic.

TUESDAY, SEPTEMBER 16TH

O God, You have made us subject to time limitations. Even though we may not like this, remind us often for our everlasting benefit.

Worked in my study, especially doing genealogical research. It seems the Lacys emerged from France during the eleventh century. Thank You, Lord, for my ancestors. Their God is my God. Their Christ is also my Christ.

Went to Phi Delta Kappa meeting at the Alumni Center on the Ball State University campus. I have been a member of the fraternity more than fifty years. Dr. Eric King, new superintendent of schools for Muncie, was the guest speaker. I gave thanks for his pastoral heart.

Often reflect on my forty-four years as a resident pastor and the many different district superintendents for whom I worked. Of the twenty-eight I would grade them as follows: Excellent—1; Good—8; Fair—11; Poor—5; and Very Poor—3. The grading is done on the basis of spiritual sensitivity, administrative know-how, and pastoral care for both churches and pastors. Too often there was the sense he was merely a "church politics" appointment and little more.

Love is patient and kind; love is not jealous or boastful; it is not arrogant or rude.

WEDNESDAY, SEPTEMBER 17TH

We are called to be holy, O Lord, and so often we don't want to be! Pull away our natural defenses and show us this spiritual splendor.

Went to Rotary in New Castle at the new Bella Vita restaurant for a gathering of community leaders to promote United Fund.

Discovered among my ancestral goodies a real gem. It was my great grandfather Walradt's New Testament, given to him by his wife on July 28, 1913. I especially prized what he had handwritten in the front: "Pure Religion—is the right adjustment of one's heart and life to God to one's self and to fellow men." He had also handwritten: "Unbelief—is the cause of all sin or foundation of it." He passed away in 1935 and is buried in the Mooreland Cemetery (Indiana). I was two years old at the time.

I believe in water baptism but find no problem in how much or how little water is used.

The number of sacraments has never been a major issue with me. I can see how there might be two or seven, yes, or the number might be something in between.

THURSDAY, SEPTEMBER 18TH

Lord of the universe, I kneel before Your unlimited power and know in my depths Your will is always done.

Dorothy and I took the afternoon off and drove to Hamilton Town Center (near Noblesville) for walking and a bit of shopping. We enjoyed ourselves and ate huge hamburgers!

Recalled with much gratitude our vacations. Special was the one we took to Washington, D.C. and beyond with all six of us. At this time, all of our girls were less than high school age. After they were grown, we made a special trip to New England where I was guest preacher in historic All Saints Anglican Church in Boston. During the same trip, we also visited where I was stationed in the U.S. Navy (Newport, Rhode Island). Among the several others, probably the leisurely trip to Yellowstone was our most enjoyable and satisfying. During that trip, much to our chagrin, she had a fall and broke some ribs!

O God, help us to keep perspective as biblical fundamentalists boldly attempt to convince us of their only right way to interpret Holy Scripture!

Anonymous good deeds, O Lord, are imperative to keep our world from destroying itself.

FRIDAY, SEPTEMBER 19TH

O Lord, keep calling our nation to repentance! Our financial predicament is only a symptom; solving it will not solve our deeper problems.

Went to Masonic Home in Franklin, Indiana to do book signing. I was given a lovely area in a spacious foyer at the administrative building. A former parishioner from Yorktown UMC, Rex Stiffler, came to me and said his wife, Marlyn, had died earlier in the night. They were residents of the home. It was a stunning moment for both of us that I would be there at that time. Just a coincidence? I doubt it.

I have always been grateful for the changing of the seasons here in Indiana. It takes some adjustment, but provides variety.

We owe so much to others. How can we repay them? Maybe we can't, but we can make attempts.

Masonic Home signing was not very productive and somewhat disappointing, but I am not complaining.

SATURDAY, SEPTEMBER 20TH

O God, much and maybe most of my life, I cannot rationally understand, but I sense a spiritual cohesiveness.

Went to Mishawaka to do a book signing for Borders. Excellent cooperation from Ryan and others. In a way, it was a strange signing with the early hours being very productive and the later ones almost totally nonproductive. Nevertheless, I touched lives and they touched mine!

When I was a very little boy, did someone rigidly and disrespectfully reject me? I can't help wondering.

The divisions among professing Christians is so hurtful, covering generations and centuries. Why, Lord?

Grateful for safe travels through confusing road construction and often heavy traffic during my book signing trip. The dear Lord rides with me!

SUNDAY, SEPTEMBER 21ST

Looking forward, O Lord, to a day of worship, sharing food with my wife and relaxation. Sometimes I suspect You spoil us!

Worshipped at Central Christian in Anderson. Brilliant presentation by the pastor, Rick Vale. People friendly.

Dorothy and I enjoyed the Texas Roadhouse. When I announced Grandma needs her steak, she knows where I am taking her!

Leisurely reading, television, and walking in the subdivision made for a beautiful and simple conclusion to the day.

Finally, concluded the late evening with the service of intercession and Holy Communion. This act of worship is so important!

MONDAY, SEPTEMBER 22ND

Keep me occupied, heavenly Father, in harmony with Your Holy Spirit. Please don't let me be bogged down in self-pity.

Spent most of the day putting newsletter together for my Associates. Believe this one completes twenty consecutive years of monthly newsletters.

My two brothers have adult children, grown and gone from home. Mike has Brad Michael and Brian Scott. Joe has Denise, Joseph Allen Junior, and Jackie. None of them resides in Indiana.

Mike and his wife live in Randolph County, Indiana (near Parker City). Joe is deceased and his wife, Monika, is still living.

Gratitude that is genuine is the source of victorious living. The presence of Jesus the Christ through the Holy Spirit is what I most sincerely value. We may seem alone, but we never are!

TUESDAY, SEPTEMBER 23RD

Saint Paul tells us to fill our minds with those things that are good and deserve praise. Enable us, Lord, to do just that!

Relaxing and rewarding moment at IHOP, having coffee and reading the *Indianapolis Star*. Waitresses were so attentive and kind.

When I get to heaven, I hope I don't have to tell my Lord in how many restaurants I drank coffee and count the number of persons with whom I visited!

Your grace, O Lord, Your grace. So much we cannot do for ourselves, especially spiritually. More and more I depend on You.

Please grant Your protective care to my family throughout the night. They are all so dear to me. Thank You!

WEDNESDAY, SEPTEMBER 24TH

Embrace Your sons and daughters, O Lord, and tell us how much You love us. It will mend our hearts and move us forward in faith.

Went to Rotary meeting for fun and fellowship. Stopped on the way at Mount Summit, Indiana, and gave away a copy of one of my books to a service station owner. These more or less spontaneous acts of ministry have been many in my life. Lord, I am not bragging!

Sat with Don Johnson of Anderson Breakfast Rotary Club, who was visiting New Castle club. He is retired from the Church of God Mission Board (Anderson).

Financial structure of our nation continues to be a major problem. Bad economic times can be painful, but the important thing is that we learn from them.

Are humility and weakness the same thing? Well, not necessarily, but the dividing line can be very thin.

THURSDAY, SEPTEMBER 25TH

My Guide and Companion! Thank You, Holy Spirit. Day and night You continually come to me. Please don't ever leave me alone.

Reflected on my longest appointment, which was Walkerton UMC (1993–1999), near South Bend. Among those who were helpful were Glenn and Lori Jacob, Jo Hershberger, Dick Reese, John and Betty Hostrawser, Harriett Klinedinst, Emma Hostetler, Mary Hahn, Sue Shields, Dan and Shirley Awald, Gerald Kaufman, Ed Vanderhoef, Gerald Hahn, Char Zwiezynski, Bob Flaugher, Mary Ann McGwin, Linda Klinedinst, Helen Hunter, Bea Seaholm, Jean Cole, Linda Craft, Jeff and Penni Fansler, Mahlon and Patty Jacob, Ray and Marian Chapman, Bob Relos, Marlyn Hochstetler, Linda Relos, and Scott and Jill Hostetler.

Koontz Lake, slightly south of Walkerton, was very interesting because of the number of Chicago people that had moved there.

I cannot imagine serving one church for ten, fifteen, or twenty years. I have always questioned an appointment of more than ten years. It seems to me to be fruitful in one place for a lengthy period, you should move elsewhere and give a new parish your time and talents, thereby strengthening an entire annual conference.

O God, continue to work through the systems of polity we have created and make us humble before Your appointive powers.

FRIDAY, SEPTEMBER 26TH

Lord, in gratitude and trust I kneel before You. When confusion comes and goes, hold me steady, Lord God.

Went to Walden's in Logansport, Indiana for book signing. Very sparse crowd but inspirational work by Jan, the manager.

Americans are focused on the financial crises in our country. Judgment may have come and will have to work itself out. Like all problems, it has a spiritual and moral dimension.

I have never lost sight of the USA being a beacon to the world. In a deep and mysterious sense, it is a chosen nation.

Relax me, O Lord, for a night of restful sleep that I may continue Your ministry wherever I am and with whomever I find myself.

SATURDAY, SEPTEMBER 27TH

Our efforts and the successes we expect, O Lord, at times are painfully frustrating. Teach us anew what really counts is our harmony with the Holy Spirit.

Off to do two more book signings, one in Greenfield and another in Indianapolis. Both fell well below expectations.

Remembered with deep appreciation my sixty-fifth birthday party at Walkerton UMC (1998). Donna (Lacy) Beyl had set up a surprise event following worship; it was beautifully engineered. A great blessing!

Also remembered the celebration of my forty years as an ordained minister at Yorktown UMC (2000). Congregation and others were so kind and gracious. It was a very special service with Lamar Imes preaching.

There is so much for which to be thankful, Lord. Every day is a good day. Some are better than others!

SUNDAY, SEPTEMBER 28TH

Sometimes, precious Lord, I feel like a little boy, who is afraid he will fail. Thank You for being the One who decides whether or not I fail!

Went to High Street UMC for worship. It was a spiritual treat for Dorothy and me to sit together in that great old church. I offer my tears of gratitude.

Went to Wilson-Shook Funeral Home in Parker City, Indiana to see Rob Hendricks, who passed away at age forty-one. He was Uncle Bob Walradth's grandson.

O Lord, I shed tears more easily in my later years. Thank You for that gift. I have needed to be able to do so for a long time.

Thank You for my life, Lord. Someday You will tell me how well I lived it. Hopefully, I will finish this earthly course, having fought the good fight.

MONDAY, SEPTEMBER 29TH

Almighty God, You have said You are to be first in our lives and we are to have no other gods before You. Keep us watchful.

An ongoing milestone remains firmly in my heart and mind in regard to the National Workshop on Christian Unity being held in Indianapolis in 1989. The theme was "Building Community: One Body in Christ." I was chair of the Ecumenical Concerns Department of Indiana Council of

Churches at the time. I had begun working on the invitation in 1984 and had secured invitational letters from key religious leaders on a statewide basis. Well, a few of us did our homework well and persisted. It has not returned to the Hoosier state and I am not sure there is the commitment in the current ecumenical climate for that to happen.

What beautiful and helpful people often grace our lives only briefly. Sometimes they inspire us to higher heights and we are uniquely blessed. I believe that is true of the NWCU, past and present.

An ecumenical education that is practical is a dire need in our contemporary world. Few seem to agree but ecumenism can be elusive and God remains in control!

Remembering with deep affection the many who have touched my life with their tears.

TUESDAY, SEPTEMBER 30TH

Purify us, O God, individually and as a nation. Help us to fall on our knees and repent of our ongoing sinfulness.

Those who profess the Christian Faith, lay and clergy, have favorite passages from the Holy Scriptures. I have read and mediated on mine countless times and believe they have strongly influenced my spiritual formation. The most basic are: Matthew chapters 5, 6, and 7 (Sermon on the Mount); Luke chapters 1 and 2 (Birth Narrative); John 6:53–58 (Holy Communion); Jeremiah chapter 1 (his call); and Micah 6:8 (text of my first sermon). There are numerous others but I believe these provide the core. I cannot imagine living my life without them!

The writings of Saints Peter, Paul, and James are always helpful. In fact, the First Epistle of Peter was utilized for my doctoral project.

The richness of our Faith in the Holy Scriptures is so marvelous and magnificent we barely get acquainted with it before the Death Angel makes plans to come and get us!

O Lamb of God, Who takes away the sins of the world, have mercy and grant us Your peace.

OCTOBER
2 0 0 8

WEDNESDAY, OCTOBER 1ST

I do so little for You, dear Lord. My efforts seem so ineffectual. Yet, I know in my depths You love me and care about me.

Please, Lord, grant that all the Lacy and Walradth families that have gone on from this earth, those who remain, and those yet to come will be saved by Your grace.

Rotary Club was again filled with fellowship. Visited with Bill Baker, an attorney, and told him of my early ambition to be one.

Recalled with appreciation the times I met our son-in-law's parents, John and Patti Graham. Both impressed me as wholesome, hard-working folks. He was a farmer and she was a teacher.

Thank You, Lord, for so many healthy opportunities that relate to people. They belong to You and they come in different sizes and shapes!

THURSDAY, OCTOBER 2ND

Bring to our memories, Lord, the love of money is the source of all kinds of evil. As Christians, keep us ever mindful of healthy conservatism.

Did preparation for my sermon at Saint Andrew Presbyterian on Sunday, October 12th. Have been led to speak about the necessity of being childlike.

My energies are churning, God, and I feel the need to be doing something, but I do not know what. Grant me a generous amount of patience!

Watched most of the Biden/Palin debate. Biden was filled with information. She was filled with a winsome relational style.

I pray the right president and vice-president will be in Washington, D.C. in January, 2009. Only You, dear God, know the right ones.

FRIDAY, OCTOBER 3RD

Give us the experience of joy, dear Lord, in our personal and public lives. We need that which is genuine and not contrived.

A morning of setting up and confirming book signings. In 2009, I expected to alter my approach with fewer travels to bookstores.

When I am gone overnight, I pray my wife and family will be protected and all go well with Your blessings.

Attended Yorktown UMC fall dinner. Met many old friends and thoroughly enjoyed ourselves. Rosemary Lillie and Toni Thomas are special.

Holy Spirit of God, please grant Your guidance in all I do and say. Grant everything is for Your glory and the salvation of precious people.

SATURDAY, OCTOBER 4TH

Nothing but the blood of Jesus! That is the way it is and has been for the two thousand years that human beings have the gift of salvation. The price was paid by Jesus the Christ.

Drove to Evansville for a book signing with Borders. While it is all interstate travel, it takes five hours from Muncie. Signing was quite productive and numerous conversations seemed to be positive. Being a longstanding UMC pastor in Indiana was helpful.

Spent the night in Evansville in a comfortable and clean motel. Watched a TV documentary on Osama bin Laden, which was very interesting and informative. Appreciated the time of being away from people and being able to ponder without interruption.

Chicago Cubs are out of the playoffs and what's new? Some of us have suffered with and for them for decades.

Southwestern Indiana for me is a wonderful place to visit, but honestly I wouldn't want to live there for very long!

SUNDAY, OCTOBER 5TH

Lord, thank You for a safe night and prospect of another fruitful time of greeting people.

Headed toward Terre Haute. Stopped in Princeton at Bob Evans for breakfast. Drove around town briefly and saw my old church building (First UMC).

Arrived at Books-A-Million in Terre Haute, near I-70. Again, the signing went well. Felt compassion for a woman, along in years, being divorced; she appeared distraught. Had the same feeling for a woman with cancer. Both bought books.

Arrived home safe and sound before 10:00 PM. This was a bonus. Thank You, Lord, for Your protective care.

Can we say without qualifications that the Christian Faith is superior to all others and if so, why?

MONDAY, OCTOBER 6TH

Thank You, Lord, for the thousands of people who have come into my life over these many years. This was not by coincidence!

A day of mostly routine computer work and telephoning. It has been good for me to do more basic tasks.

Bought a birthday card for my brother Mike, who was sixty-five yesterday. I also picked up a Sears gift card for him.

Please remember, dear Lord, our pastors who are under heavy pressure by their laity. We must stand firmly but kindly.

I want the happiness only You, Jesus, the Christ my Savior and Lord can give. Yes, when I am weak, I am strong and rightly dependent on the Holy Spirit.

TUESDAY, OCTOBER 7TH

Stretch me, O Lord, and make me grow in ways You deem best. I shall seek to be resilient and open to Your Holy Spirit.

Treated my brother Mike to his birthday breakfast at IHOP. We had a healthy time of sharing and caring.

It seems almost daily I receive inspirational cards, letters, and labels from Roman Catholic organizations. I am appreciative.

We cannot all be saints, dear Lord, but we can all on occasion be saintly. Remind us of our true vocation: to be Christian in fact and not merely theory.

Please, dear Lord, protect my loved ones throughout the night. Give them a new day tomorrow and walk by their sides.

WEDNESDAY, OCTOBER 8TH

At all costs hold to God's unchanging hand. Our Father will guide and protect us, all of us, at junctures in our lives.

Rotary meeting had a Young Life speaker, who was mature and evidenced the spirit of Christ. May God's blessings rest upon him.

Reflected on major formative years in my professional life (1974–1979) at Seymour First UMC, where I did my DMIN work. Key folks were Glenn Seward, Paul Bell, Tom Johnson, Hugh Grim, David McFall, Ed Whitcomb (former governor of Indiana) and his family, Ken Warbritton, Charles and Thelma Lisman, Pat Baxter, Liz Sparks, Joe and Nancy Erp, Jane Nowlin, Dorothy Myers, Carolyn Gordon, Guy Ramsey (retired UMC pastor), Harry and Luellen Rolf, Mitzi Durham, Charles Conquest, Charles Linke, Scott Sunbury, Earl Prout, Ed Boley, Sara Beck, Louis Abraham Sr., and John Bottorff.

It has been my ongoing desire to communicate to the congregations and constituents I have served that I care about them and appreciate them. While many have gone the way of all flesh, there is the communion of saints.

Call us to be merciful, Lord, and give us patience that we may live peaceably among those not so patient!

THURSDAY, OCTOBER 9TH

Keep us ever grateful, O Lord, for those who have loved us and cared for us. They are like shining stars in the heavens.

Except for book signing preparation, it was a slow and relaxing day. I have learned to appreciate such days and not seek to be busy for the sake of being busy!

We went to see grandson Fillip's football game in Fishers. It was a thriller, but his team lost by six points. It was an evening well spent and he was very glad to see us there. He is such a good-looking and well-mannered lad.

As the financial crisis seems to deepen, remind us, Lord, of Your wisdom and power. We thank You for Your ongoing care.

I have been trying to remember my first little girlfriend at Blountsville School (Indiana). Believe it was Joy Lee Brown in the second grade.

FRIDAY, OCTOBER 10TH

Cause us never to lose heart, O God, and may we rest assured in Your providence. Guide us always, even among the most mundane things of life, into faithful participation for Your Kingdom.

Went to a signing at Family Christian Book Store in Greenwood. Met Chris, the manager, and he was quick to get me started. Flow of people was erratic, but made some sales to those who were obviously blessed by our interaction.

The Holy Spirit walks with me and talks with me and tells me I belong to Christ the Lord.

Quick and safe return home. Felt a sense of accomplishment and peace of mind.

Never thought much about living beyond my early eighties. Maybe God will allow me into the late eighties or more.

SATURDAY, OCTOBER 11TH

Father, Son, and Holy Spirit, I welcome this day with gratitude, hope and promise.

Went to Family Christian Book Store in Muncie to present a special event. For the first time, I am offering eleven different book titles. Conversations were many and positive. Among those coming were Bob Robinson (retired judge), Joe and Dorothy Duncan, George Harris, and Jim and Joann Beckley. Sales were above average. One couple bought four different titles! *Methodist Mass*, a collectors item, received considerable attention from several people.

How shall we escape if we neglect so great a salvation? That question needs to be asked daily at every social level of our society.

Trying to think of some young women I would have considered marrying before Dorothy came into my life. Frankly, I have not come up with any names and probably won't.

Some folks have a problem with Freemasonry. I don't and doubt that I will in the future.

SUNDAY, OCTOBER 12TH

Obedience, Lord, is imperative and not obedience to something or someone not of Your choosing. Keep us pure and undefiled.

Preached at Saint Andrew Presbyterian. Built my theme around something my granddaughter Natalie Rene had done last May. On her third birthday, as she was coming down a flight of stairs to the party, she pleaded with her father, Jeffrey, to come and get her. She needed her father's special presence, protection, and assurances. I used Saint Matthew's text, 18:1–5. We are called to be childlike. To do so means the following characteristics are present: innocence, dependence, honest, sincerity, and patience. The congregation loved it!

Sometimes it is so difficult for us to get through the years and layers of formal education to become childlike.

Guest preaching has always been a delight for me. I cannot remember a bad experience.

Often, Lord, our cares are many in spite of the fact You have told us not to worry.

MONDAY, OCTOBER 13TH

I kneel before Your greatness, O God, and pause in sincere gratitude for Your continuing care of my family and myself.

Please remember our two sons-in-law, Terry Beyl and Jeffrey Graham. We cherish them as husbands and fathers.

Federal offices were closed because of it being Columbus Day. I worked mostly in my study and on the Internet.

Dear Lord, I am deeply concerned about Dorothy. Her health seems to be failing rather rapidly. I want to be good to her.

Sunday's sermon continues to linger in my heart and mind. The Holy Spirit used me and gave the congregation a gift, thanks be to God.

TUESDAY, OCTOBER 14TH

O Lord, grant me more humility in my coming and going. You know just the right amount, so I trust You.

Special mailings made that involved my literary and ecumenical ministries. Lord, thank You for the financial resources to do such things.

I took Dorothy to Castleton Square in Indianapolis for an afternoon and evening of relaxation. It was a good time!

There is much envy in this tired, old world, dear Lord. It seems to be lurking most everyplace I find myself. Help all afflicted out of this pit!

Telephone conversation with Bill Ryon out in Virginia helpful to bring the ministry of our Ecumenical Society of the Blessed Virgin Mary into perspective.

WEDNESDAY, OCTOBER 15TH

Your Kingdom, O Lord, is now and yet forever. Help us to understand Your sheer eternal greatness.

Rotary meeting program was a travelogue presented by Dave Burns and his wife. It was an excellent program, featuring Tunisia.

Some heartaches in our Rotary club. I will pray for them individually and personally. They, in a way, are my people!

Watched the third and final debate between Obama and McCain. It was McCain's best outing. I was proud of the old guy!

Please keep my loved ones safe throughout the night, Lord. You are the only one who can truly do that.

THURSDAY, OCTOBER 16TH

How happy the saints must be in heaven! Some of us, dear Lord, in our own little ways of giving and living hope to join them some day.

Thank You, Lord, for our little home. It is both comfortable and convenient. In some ways it is better than anything I thought we would ever have.

The day was mostly marked by using the Internet and culling book signing worksheets. What needed to be done for the moment was done.

A very important, even crucial, lesson has been taught to me, my Lord: the head must find its way into the heart.

I have never thought of myself as a well-rounded person in the human sense. Such matters for me always have a spiritual dimension, fully known only to God.

FRIDAY, OCTOBER 17TH

God bless America, land that I love, stand beside her and guide her through the night with a light from above.

Went to Marion, Indiana to do a book signing at the Tree of Life Bookstore. Impressive, small, and evangelical environs. The Holy Spirit was indeed present. Students from Indiana Wesleyan University came by the dozens. Even though they purchased very little, I was inspired by the students' presence! There was an excellence about them.

Returned home before 9:00 PM, which was a bonus and I know Dorothy appreciated it.

Son-in-law Terry has been on my mind for some hours now. He has been a vigorous, golf-playing, and professional type of guy. The family loves him.

Recalled my closing words to Saint Paul UMC in Rushville. I moved away from the feel good stuff and told them the truth!

SATURDAY, OCTOBER 18TH

The riches of the Faith are barely tapped, O Lord. Please help all of us who profess the Faith to do better, much better.

Went to northwest Indianapolis to do book signing for Books-A-Million. The distributor failed to deliver, so I used my own supply. Splendid signing! Both the flow of people and their openness to my greeting them were prize-winning. It seemed several were there who had connections to Saint Luke's UMC (Indianapolis). This was helpful because I know some of the staff there. We sold out of books, so needless to say, I went happily home! I could not even remotely see that success coming.

Reflected with thankful memories of good times Jim Willyard and I shared together. Jim was a UMC pastor for nearly forty years. He passed away in his early sixties. We roomed together at the School of the Prophets (DePauw University) and at annual conferences. He had been an associate pastor at High Street UMC in Muncie and I held a similar position at College Avenue UMC in the same city.

Friendships in the ministry with those in the same denomination can be precarious. That's why ecumenical relationships can be very rewarding.

I apologize and repent to God for anyone I failed to serve adequately in all of my churches.

SUNDAY, OCTOBER 19TH

Thank You, Lord, for High Street UMC! That great, old church, indeed, Muncie's Methodist Cathedral, gave me a wonderful place to worship during my college years. While worshipping there today, old appreciations returned with a blessed spiritual aroma.

Dorothy and I shared our noon meals at the Olive Garden. The waitress, Meghan, was kind, courteous, and efficient.

In the afternoon, all of our little family came for the Christmas drawing of names. We watched football on television and we had some tasty refreshments.

I like to remind people Christmas is a holy day and not a holiday. Maybe we Americans should give fewer presents and get along better together!

If I have failed to serve anyone adequately in all of the churches I pastored, I repent to the Living God.

MONDAY, OCTOBER 20TH

Pray and pray some more during these days. Our nation and world, dear Lord, are in need of Your loving powers.

Spent the morning bringing my various ministries up-to-date. So grateful I have been able to develop meaningful ministry beyond the confines of the pastorate.

Sometimes I talk when I should have been listening. Surely, Lord, You can supply me with more patience.

Worked on my monthly Associates newsletter. The letter had its inception in October of 1988. I have published every month since then.

I finally have the sense, O Lord, that I totally and completely belong to You. Do I have any free will left?

TUESDAY, OCTOBER 21ST

Come by here, Lord. O Lord, come by here. Someone is praying, Lord. Someone is crying, Lord. Someone needs You, Lord. Someone is singing, Lord.

During our lives, once in awhile, the Holy Spirit comes into our midst and we are blessed beyond words. How grateful we are, O Lord.

Went to Richmond and was the guest speaker for the Rotary Club. In a pastoral way I gave a talk about gaining new members. The meeting was handled well by a young banker. I appreciated the kindness and questions. It was time well spent.

Keep preparing us for death, dear Lord, for surely we shall all take the voyage. Some of us like to think of it as a graduation.

Through their Wesleyan heritage, Methodists have produced some great men and women. Yet, Lord, that is only part of the one, holy, catholic, apostolic Church and insist, Lord, we remember that.

WEDNESDAY, OCTOBER 22ND

Continue to fill me with Your Spirit, Lord. It makes a qualitative difference in my life and in others as well. Inspire me and enable me to forgive everyone who has wronged me. Genuine forgiveness carries the day (and night) for all of us.

Went to Rotary in New Castle and sat with friends. The club is blessed with a spirit of caring and sharing. I continue to offer my prayers for them.

Dorothy and I took the evening off and headed for the Gas City, Indiana, exit. We feasted there on Cracker Barrel's food! This exit has developed into a major restaurant, motel, and service station stop on I-69. It is a gateway to both Taylor and Indiana Wesleyan Universities.

I spoke to the faculty and students at Taylor in January 1984. It was the Week of Prayer for Christian Unity.

O Lord, we have been faithful over a few things and trust we can spend eternity with You.

THURSDAY, OCTOBER 23RD

In the name of the Father, Son, and Holy Spirit. Three persons in one God. One God in three persons. Blessed Trinity.

O Your matchless wonders, Lord! You are always the difference in our lives and I praise Your holy name!

My human weakness, Lord, is blatantly obvious. My ongoing need of You is even more obvious! Without You, Lord, I become nothing.

Received two unexpected phone calls inviting me to do book signings. One was in New Castle and the other in Terre Haute. Pleased to accept them.

Thank You, Lord, for my prayer life. It really became of primary importance during my pastorate at Leesburg UMC.

FRIDAY, OCTOBER 24TH

While I am moving along in years, Lord, I know there is still much for me to do for You either in person or in writing.

Reflected on my last full-time appointment at Yorktown UMC, near the west edge of Muncie. Such beautiful and mature people! Among the many prize laity were Max Shideler, Darrel Hughes, Ron and Cheryl Fauquher, Tim and Carol Spangler, Dave and Suzi Ober, Rosemary Lillie, Toni Thomas, Dave Parkison, Joe and Joy Grady, Randy and Cindy Sollars, Walt and Carolyn Ellison, Dick Groves, Earl and Louise Luke, Thelma King, John and Barb Chaille, Virginia Mercer, Gene Finley, Jim Beedle, Phil and Sue Bonneau, Frank and Janet Burrows, Mary Jo Estep, Peg Flanagan, Jewel Hancock, Gary Reese, Eddie and Virginia Richcreek, Judy St. John, Dorothy Thornburg, Rex and Marlyn Stiffler, Charles and Madalyn Ayres, Sue Parkinson, and Carole Young. The list could grow very long and perhaps include the entire membership of nearly four hundred people. At any rate, I thank all of them!

In surveying all of the churches I have served over the years, nearly all have lost a considerable number of members. For example, at the time I was at Hagerstown First UMC, it had six hundred plus members, but today is barely half that amount.

Are we near the second coming of Christ? Perhaps, but only God knows for sure, and it has not happened yet!

A love that has no limits excites and inspires me, Lord, but I don't have it. We must continually look to You for that magnificence!

SATURDAY, OCTOBER 25TH

O Lord, Lamb of God, Who takes away the sins of the world, have mercy. I beg of You, please forgive our nation's sins.

Went to Columbus, Ohio to do a book signing at Barnes and Noble in the northwestern part of the city. It turned out to be an above-average signing in both sales and conversations. There are a lot of good people out there!

Arrived at Red Roof Inn for the night. It was near a Bob Evans, which was helpful. Watched the ongoing presidential debates on television. Fox network seems to be the only major network seriously providing balanced viewpoints.

The knowledge I have gained from being on the road with signings is fascinating and has given me new perspectives. These are unique educational experiences, which have come largely in retirement. I give thanks!

After preaching virtually every Sunday for about fifty years, I am learning new styles of ministry and am blessed.

SUNDAY, OCTOBER 26TH

How good You are to me, O Lord! The previous night was relaxing and I sensed a special peace.

Leisurely breakfast at Bob Evans. Immensely enjoyed the *Columbus Dispatch*. It may be a cut above the *Indianapolis Star*.

Went to Pickerington, south and east of Columbus, to do another signing. It was also Barnes and Noble. Very supportive staff, especially the manager, and excellent promotion of my books. Some truly inspirational moments with persons I had never seen before, which is typical.

It does not seem possible the years that have passed and the literally thousands of people I have met and known. As we walk hand-in-hand with God, He has a way of surprising us.

Returned home before 11:00 PM, which was amazing, considering the distance. I celebrated a worthwhile and rewarding trip.

MONDAY, OCTOBER 27TH

Help us to remember in the depths of our beings, Lord: Jesus saves by His crucifixion and we find salvation in Him. Here is powerful love!

Recalled my relationship with Dick Groves at Yorktown UMC. His history of the local church was a real gift. Dick's many kindnesses are not at all forgotten.

Morning was filled with catching up in my office. Thanks so much, Lord, for the numerous opportunities to serve others.

Delighted with having both of the new journals from the North and South Annual Conferences UMC, here in Indiana. Exploring people and statistics held my intense interest!

Please be especially close to our son-in-law Terry Beyl dear Lord. He has been and is so good to all of us. We appreciate him so much.

TUESDAY, OCTOBER 28TH

Continue to enlighten me, O Lord, in Your holy ways. Purify and sanctify me and my motives.

Gave thanks for the letters received from Marvin and Dottie Culy of Hagerstown First UMC long after I ceased to be their pastor. Such unsolicited words of caring are worth more than money can buy!

A day of reading and reflecting. Some of my pastoral appointments were, indeed, painful and yet subtly fruitful! God always knows our real needs.

Thought often about my immediate family and how much I have loved them and continue to do so, perhaps even more so. Trusting in God to care for them, long after I am gone.

Returned telephone call to James Earl Massey, a truly great preacher, from the Church of God (Anderson). His voice, Christian devotion, and homiletical skills are simply marvelous.

WEDNESDAY, OCTOBER 29TH

Just to be counted among the redeemed, O Lord, is truly a blessing beyond full description. Mold me and make me Your own.

My wife and I decided to take the full day off, so we drove to Fort Wayne. It was a gorgeous, sunny day. We had a sumptuous lunch at Sara's restaurant and then went to Jefferson Pointe for walking, shopping, and relaxation. Having our fill there, we drove to spacious Glenbrook Mall. It may very well be the most attractive and complete mall in Indiana. After a Bob Evans outing, we came home. Both of us considered it a good day and congratulated each other!

I seek to pray each day for my United Methodist brothers in ministry. We never know what is in the lives of others, except as the Holy Spirit shows us.

It is crucial in the ministry not to rust out, but victoriously to wear out. In various ways, we are all given the gifts of time, energy, and talent.

There is a question few are willing to ask, at least openly: will the overly-feminizing of our society and culture eventually bring us to ruin?

THURSDAY, OCTOBER 30TH

It's not brother nor my sister, O Lord, standing in the need of prayer. It is me, O Lord. It is me!

It began as a troublesome day with tension and pressure. There appeared to be more than one cause, but only God knows for sure. Depression seemed unrelenting and then it lifted after a trip to the local library. A phone call from a laywoman at Saint Andrew Presbyterian also helped.

I ran out of Kosher Communion wine, so I picked up a bottle for my morning and night private services.

Late evening walk was helpful in clearing the confusion and anger from my heart and mind. The devil is clever!

Trusting all Christians throughout the world are keeping the Faith. So many in America who profess the Faith know so little about real sacrifice.

FRIDAY, OCTOBER 31ST

O Lord, inspire and enable my Catholic friends here and those around the world to practice their Faith with diligence. So much depends on Catholics to show us the way in living the life Christ wants us to live.

Keep us praying, Lord, for the United States of America. We want Your president and Your vice-president elected.

Thank You, God, for this great nation and the freedom I have along with others. I beg of You, stay close during this election.

Long ago, I reveled in the teaching of American history and my patriotism has not diminished. We are a special people called to be a beacon to the world and that is not egotistical nationalism!

Today was mostly one of pondering and impatiently waiting for that which, as yet, has not come about.

NOVEMBER
2 0 0 8

SATURDAY, NOVEMBER 1ST

Thank You, Lord, for human relationships to help us along the way. Sometimes I need to take the initiative in an unselfish way.

It was a day of sitting with our grandchildren Natalie Rene and Justin Daniel Graham. Dorothy bore the load of the day, but I assisted and helped supply energy. We were with them a full twelve hours. Martha and Jeff, their parents, had gone to a football game at Notre Dame in South Bend. Jeff did his undergraduate work there. Notre Dame lost in four overtimes!

We arrived home safe and sound with Grandmother Lacy being extremely tired. I gave thanks for a day well-spent.

Only God knows how, why, and when the generations come and go. I believe our prayers need to be for those in the past, present, and future.

When being close to Notre Dame during my Walkerton UMC pastorate (1993–1999), I always appreciated the connections with the university.

SUNDAY, NOVEMBER 2ND

Amazing Grace, how great and awesome are your victories! Do for us what we can never do for ourselves.

Gave humble thanks for those who made the Lacy Institute for Ecumenism Scholarship at Christian Theological Seminary a reality. Charter members included: Dr. Gene E. Sease, William L. Ryon Jr., Rev. James W. Beckley, Dr. Ronald W. Liechty, Honorable Evan D. Goodman, Dr. David R. Cartwright, Deacon James K. MacDougall, Randy J. Sollars, Rev. Stephen M. Bard, Donald P. Hilbert, Charles Kirklin, Dr. and Mrs. John E. Weakland, Dr. and Mrs. Gary L. Reif, Dr. and Mrs. David Ober, Earl Luke, Wade D. Rubick,

Mr. and Mrs. Ralph E. Bushey, Mr. and Mrs. Joseph E. Grady, Mr. and Mrs. Barry Wampler, Dr. Terril Littrell, Rev. Dan Motto, and myself. It also needs to be noted that Indiana Partners for Christian Unity and Mission made a generous gift, which was an inspirational surprise! IPCUM is the successor to the Indiana Council of Churches.

Trusting in God that the LIFE scholarships will be beneficial for those who receive them. My *Decalogue for Ecumenical Discipleship* is the basis for awarding them.

Sometimes we have to learn that prosperity and secular success can lead us to most any place, except where God wants us to go!

Dear God, help us to remember all Your benefits and blessings, even those that come to us in pain-filled moments.

MONDAY, NOVEMBER 3RD

The Holy Scriptures, Lord! We are called to immerse our lives in them and seek to practice all they tell us.

Forgive us, Lord, for reading many things carefully, except the Holy Scriptures. Please call Your people to a better pathway.

Believe little—tiny by most standards—Center High School in Perry Township of Delaware County (Indiana) imparted solid, practical wisdom to most of us. Remembered with great appreciation high school teachers who contributed to my life: E. K. Keesling and James McJilton.

Watched Fox News, CNN, and others attempting to prepare us for election day and the ensuing results. O God, grant Your will be done and ways prevail.

As a boy, like everyone else, I could not perceive the unfolding of my life and yet there was a glimpse now and then.

TUESDAY, NOVEMBER 4TH

All powerful, all knowing, and ever present God, we go to the polls today to elect a new president and vice-president.

We continue to pray that Your will be done and Your ways prevail. Our nation is moving into a different time of history, perhaps of a radical nature.

Changes are emerging all about us and, truthfully, we are sometimes frightened. We need, Lord, Your loving but firm presence.

Lord, I am a patriot with religious fervor and have been all my life. God and country belong together!

Precious Lord, hold my hand. Indeed, hold our nation's hand and lead us in Your pathways and to Your destinations.

WEDNESDAY, NOVEMBER 5TH

Let us give thanks to our God and especially thank him for our Savior and Lord, Jesus the Christ.

Went to a congenial and satisfying breakfast meeting for retired UMC clergy. We all showed wear and tear!

Glad to be back at New Castle Rotary meeting. Girls basketball coach of New Castle High School was the speaker. Sense of belonging to oneself and giving of ministry among those Rotarians. Grateful the Lord has seen fit to use me in this way.

Barack Obama is our newly-elected president and Joe Biden our new vice-president.

O God, grant Your will be done and Your ways prevail. Our nation is moving into mostly uncharted waters and, yes, we really need You.

THURSDAY, NOVEMBER 6TH

Thank You, Lord, for all that has been, is and shall be. Your faithfulness gives stability to my life and always has.

Today is our forty-ninth wedding anniversary. It doesn't seem possible. Lord, thank You for those years. I gave my wife a Precious Moments ornament, card, and treated us to a lavish evening at Bravos in Indianapolis.

Of the more than four hundred weddings I performed, I tried to impress upon their hearts and minds their vows were not only to one another, but before God as well. This is the essence of the sacramental nature of marriage.

I beg of You, Lord, to inspire Christians, as well as others across the world to marry and be faithful to one another. In this nation, we seem to be drowning in adultery!

Today is also the birthday of my father, Charles William Lacy. He would have been ninety-six. He was a genuinely good man in the highest and best sense of the word.

FRIDAY, NOVEMBER 7TH

Lord Jesus, lover of my soul, cause me ever to seek Your holiness for the benefit of others.

Went to Barnes and Noble in Plainfield for a book signing. It was above average in every way. Gratifying. It was in this store the *Indianapolis Star*, some months earlier, took my picture with an interview.

A pastoral journey in my life occurred after retirement. I was called into being the supply pastor of Madison Street UMC in Muncie from 2004 to 2006. It had been a major influence on the south side several years earlier and could seat five hundred people. I often preached to less than forty! Nevertheless, there were loyal folks there and among them were Bob and Mary Ann Robinson, Janel McClellan, Dennis Fisher, Joe and Catherine Fisher, Max and Dee Foster, Jim and Jenny Burgess, Betty Baughman, Ed Williams, Ruth Hodson, and Elmer West.

While I may be better known for my emphasis on ecumenism, preaching and the writing of sermons have always been a forte.

To be in good health and to do what I do are certainly gifts from God. I only seek to make use of the opportunities.

SATURDAY, NOVEMBER 8TH

Unto You, O God, we offer our prayers, well aware every word, thought, and feeling are received, considered, and recorded.

Went to Books-A-Million in Kokomo to do a book signing. It was a cold and damp day. Flow of people was spasmodic and many were not spending any money at all. Signing was sub par in sales. However, a very unusual experience did develop. A woman for whom I performed her first marriage in 1963 bought a book! I was at Kokomo Trinity UMC at the time.

It seems wisdom is gained slowly among us clergy and I think sometimes it's because of our pride. We are supposed to be more mature than we actually are!

Why did God call me into the ordained ministry? I don't really have an answer to that question, but I have never doubted that He did.

Arrived home from Kokomo before 9:30 PM, and was glad I did. My wife was not feeling well and I was able to be of at least some assistance.

SUNDAY, NOVEMBER 9TH

Your wonders abound, O God! Indeed, why do You care about us? We have need of You, but You have no need of us to continue being God.

Went to Borders in Greenwood to do book signing. Conversations were inspirational and book sales meaningful. Even though John Thompson was not working, the staff was very helpful. Overall, store sales were down, but optimism was in the air. South Indy suburbs are quite different from other sides of the city. There seems to be a more friendly attitude and even a greater spiritual sensitivity. The book stores, like this one, reflect that.

There have been so many helpful folks, in my book signings, regardless of where they are, and I give thanks for all of them.

Holy Spirit of God abide, provide, and guide me in all comings and goings. Grant I would unconditionally be Your person.

Trip home was quick and I gave thanks for another event with safe travels. Prayer has been a constant activity during these times, usually with spoken words.

MONDAY, NOVEMBER 10TH

O compassionate God, please care for my loved ones. Sometimes I don't show them my love often enough. Help me to improve.

A morning of putting things in order, following three days of book signings. Special notes of thanks to store managers are imperative.

Believe McCain could have won the election through the electoral college, simply by taking two million votes or so from Obama in key states. Had he done so, Obama would still have something like four million more popular votes. Talk about a gigantic problem! I believe it was fortunate we did not have to deal with that.

Even with our enormous wealth as a nation, we are only generous and hardly sacrificial. We want to share and do so with countless of billions of dollars, but who among us can say we have given up something very important that others may have enough?

Lord, You are the great Shepherd of the sheep. Please lead us to care for one another in ways that inspire still others.

TUESDAY, NOVEMBER 11TH

Forgive us, Lord, for being too concerned about food, drink, clothing, and shelter. Always inspire us to seek the Kingdom of God first.

We have grown so used to affluence that our spiritual senses have been dulled. Please, Lord, help us out of our predicament.

Read daily papers today more carefully than usual. Thank You, Lord, for the Catholic stand against abortion.

Help me, Lord, to be more warm and open to people. Surely I can do so without a personality change suggested by unfriendly types!

There is so much for which to be grateful. Forgive, O Lord, the many Americans who suffer from ingratitude.

WEDNESDAY, NOVEMBER 12TH

Lord, have mercy. Christ, have mercy. Lord, have mercy. Without Your mercy, we shall surely fail and fall into an abyss.

Went to Rotary meeting and greatly enjoyed the fellowship. Award-winning wrestling coach of New Castle High School was the speaker. Chief of police was a visitor at the meeting. I learned he had married a former parishioner of mine and a friend of our daughters, Kim Lyskowinski, from Seymour First UMC. Her father was principal of Seymour High School at the time.

Took my wife to MCL in Muncie for evening meal. Delicious! We look forward to such times together.

Give continual thanks for the numerous number of people I have known over the years.

Purge our nation, Lord, of its countless sins but, I beg of You, show us mercy and do not forsake us.

THURSDAY, NOVEMBER 13TH

We beg of You, Father, to continue to hold before us the call to be one. Unless Christians are united, how can the world believe?

Recalled with gratitude colleagues Sister Florette, Father Tom Baima, Father Phil Bowers, Jon Walters, Midge Roof, John Gaus, Tom Schmidt, Sister Ancilla, Mildred Artes, George J. Sheridan, Robert Coval, Tom Prinz, Margaret Orr Thomas, Monsignor Joseph C. Shenrock, Gerald F. Moede,

Paul F. Perry, Myron Yonker, John Roof, Bert C. Mulroy, Howard C. Olsen, and Sister Agnes Louise Paulus. Each contributed to my ecumenical education, among others, in various positive ways. Father Bowers baptized our granddaughter Natalie Rene Graham.

Visited by phone with old friend John R. Parks. He is a retired UMC pastor near Hartford City, Indiana. We have respected one another for forty years.

Shall we ever be able to thank all the people who made an important imprint on our lives? I doubt it, at least not in this life!

Dear Lord, please keep our little family safe throughout the night. Grant us a good day tomorrow. In thanksgiving for all your blessings.

FRIDAY, NOVEMBER 14TH

All hail the power of Jesus' name! Indeed, in Him we find our salvation for the here and now and forever.

Trip to Family Christian Book Store on northeast side of Fort Wayne was made especially enjoyable by stopping at my favorite restaurant, Bob Evans. Signing was good news/bad news. Tina, the manager, was very helpful, but flow of people and sales were sporadic. Quality conversations with two pastors, one the Church of Christ and the other Pentecostal, were encouraging. Interestingly, *Collected Works* sold well.

Began to enumerate the funeral homes in which I officiated funerals. Really, I don't remember a difficult service. Of course, some were better than others. Certainly both Meeks and Parsons in Muncie were in all ways quality. Yet, there were several others I remember with special appreciation.

Does anyone ever want to talk about hell, except in a humorous way? It certainly doesn't seem like it!

Keep calling us to be humble, Lord. Otherwise, we are not going to be teachable and that is a huge problem!

SATURDAY, NOVEMBER 15TH

Your love, Lord, Your love. The preciousness of it is beyond any tabulation or even estimation we are able to make.

My wife and I treated ourselves to an IHOP breakfast. We also visited with Al (retired UMC pastor) and Carol Kundenreich.

Went to Walden's at Mounds Mall in Anderson. Lots of people moving about. Relatively few came into the bookstore. No matter the sales numbers, I am convinced God's will is being done through these events and give humble thanks.

Amazing grace, how sweet the sound that saved a wretch like me! Onward under the banner of Jesus the Christ.

Pondered the history of the Universal Church, as I know it. So much I simply don't know.

SUNDAY, NOVEMBER 16TH

O God, I thank You over and over again for Your presence in my life and others. Where would we be without You? Oblivion!

Left for Florence, Kentucky before 8:00 AM to do a book signing at Barnes and Noble bookstore. Snowflakes along the way. The trip on Highway 3 from Muncie to New Castle and Rushville to Interstate 74 brings back many memories for me. Generous support from the bookstore's staff. Sales were mediocre. Lengthy conversations were quite revealing and very interesting.

Returned home before 11:00 PM, safe and sound. My dear Lord always rides with me. Maybe it is because I always invite Him!

Dear Lord, please be with those at Florence with whom I conversed, especially the fellow who still wants to be a Roman Catholic priest.

Can we, who profess the Christian faith, gain inspiration and insight from reading the Koran? Perhaps, but be careful!

MONDAY, NOVEMBER 17TH

Dear God, I believe in one, holy, catholic, apostolic Church. Thank You for Christ's Body of believers on earth and in heaven.

Went to Plymouth, Indiana for meeting of the Christian Unity Committee North Indiana Conference (UMC). Jon Gosser and Ron Liechty also present. To be ordained Christian pastors and yet have such differing views is truly amazing! Only God can fully understand.

O Lord, keep me ever humbly obedient to Your Holy Spirit, as I seek to do Your bidding on the ecumenical trail.

Your protective powers, dear Lord, over and over save me from auto accidents. Thank You. Thank You. Thank You.

At one time considered retiring in Plymouth, but the final appointment to Yorktown changed that.

TUESDAY, NOVEMBER 18TH

It is in silence and solitude, O Lord, we most clearly hear Your voice. Cause us to seek such times and places.

Long lunch and conversation with John R. Parks. He is a man of considerable wisdom, who does not readily show his gifts.

I have been privileged to hold ordination in the Methodist and then United Methodist Church for nearly fifty years. I am very grateful.

Retirement in many ways has been satisfying. Yet, I want to accomplish and contribute more—some days much more!

My prayers go up to You, Lord, on behalf of those already suffering from our weak economy. Inspire Your people to be generous to the less fortunate.

WEDNESDAY, NOVEMBER 19TH

Help me, Lord, to be more of a servant for others. Sometimes my self-interest and promotional ability strike a negative, divisive chord.

Another good day at New Castle Rotary. What a blessing those folks have been and are! I sense so much good happening.

Well, my depression comes and goes. The living God always remains, permanent and close. As usual, Lord, I cling to You.

Continue to recall quality funeral homes in which I had services. Flanner and Buchanan (Indianapolis), Burns (Hobart), Sollar-Baker (Lafayette), Gray (Hagerstown), Alexander (Evansville), Pasco (Greenfield), Rannels (Koontz Lake), Leppert (Indianapolis), Conkle (Indianapolis), Shirley Brothers (Indianapolis), Ellers (Kokomo), Hippensteel (Lafayette), Macer-Hall (New Castle), McHatton-Sadler (Warsaw), Johnson-Danielson (Plymouth), Moster (Rushville), Voss (Seymour), Wellsheimer (South Bend), Grossman-Good (Argos), Nusbaum-Elkin (Walkerton), and Titus (Warsaw).

Tomorrow will come and I expect to be a better person in the likeness of Jesus the Christ, Savior and Lord.

THURSDAY, NOVEMBER 20TH

We beg of You, Lord, to be close to the United States of America. We all need You, Lord, come by here!

Repentance and forgiveness can flow smoothly. But real and permanent change in our hearts can be most difficult.

Spent much of the day working on my regular column for the *Star Press* (Muncie). It seemed to take more polishing than usual.

Mailed Thanksgiving cards to several of my colleagues. I have always enjoyed doing this sort of thing.

I give thanks for Your grace, O Lord, and seek always to be one of Your sons, sinful though I am.

FRIDAY, NOVEMBER 21ST

O man of God, arise from your kneeling position with humble grace and prepare for action.

Made my way to Dayton area (Miamisburg) to do book signing at the Family Christian Book Store. Profitable time was spent with people and books. One of the persons working in the store bought two copies!

Traveling home I almost met with a major car accident. My Lord and protector provided a way of escape.

These signings have become virtually a retirement ministry and for that I give thanks. Altogether, there have now been two hundred twenty-five.

Let the healing waters flow, O great Physician! For many years, I have given thanks for being a chaplain in the International Order of Saint Luke the Physician.

SATURDAY, NOVEMBER 22ND

I need to be loved, O Lord, first by You and then by my family and other loved ones. Thank You for everyone and everything.

Went to New Castle for the area-wide author fair. Twenty-three were present in the spacious auditorium of the public library. Considering the promotion of the event, plus the diversity and quality of the authors, attendance was surprisingly really poor. I did, however, sell several copies, but others did not do nearly as well. My table was next to a lovely, cultured and elderly author Mary Anne Barothy who had worked for the *Indianapolis Star.*

Often I marvel at the movies being shown on television. Who in his right mind would want to sit through some of them?

Today marks the day in 1963 of JFK's assassination. On that day and at that time, I was in Marion, Indiana in the college library working on Sunday's sermon for my Kokomo Trinity UMC congregation.

Regardless of your mood, seek to be close to God and He'll be close to you.

SUNDAY, NOVEMBER 23RD

Thank You, Lord, for my being able to sit in a pew for Sunday morning worship. Well, maybe I have earned that right!

Saint Andrew Presbyterian folks are always welcoming. Dorothy and I appreciate their kindness and fellowship.

We shared our noon meal at Ruby Tuesday's and enjoyed it immensely. I am very grateful for my retirement income.

Spent most of the afternoon preparing materials for the Associates mailing. There seems to be no end to what is relevant!

In thanksgiving, I look to the heavens and praise God from Whom all blessings flow. Amen. Amen. Amen.

MONDAY, NOVEMBER 24TH

Thank You, Lord, for being present during a busy day. When I do not think consciously of You, I still know You are there.

Wrote Associates newsletter page and did photocopying at Staples. Put together a mailing of fourteen pages for each packet. Trip to Yorktown Post Office in late afternoon finished my project. Associates network in its twenty-first year.

Often think of Anne Marie and especially the inspirational funeral service Father William Mannion gave us. Thank You, Lord Jesus. Father Mannion was so kind and caring; he obviously understood a great deal more than he was telling us.

Dorothy and I spent the evening watching a three hour Eastwood movie about a young female boxer. It was a gem!

Mothers with children from both husbands *and* boyfriends are pursuing an ever-frightening course. Father, forgive them and give us a new day with such mothers counting the cost of their style of living and the consequences. Holy Mary, Mother of God!

TUESDAY, NOVEMBER 25TH

Yes, we reap what we sow. Sometimes there are great surprises because we do not realize at the moment when we are sowing and when we are reaping.

Breakfast with my brother Mike. He has been having some health problems, so I was especially glad to share time with him.

Did routine administrative and promotional work. I have learned this is also God's work and we are to do it with spiritual discernment.

Looking forward to Thanksgiving Day with our little family coming home. As Dorothy prepares for them, her energies are being strained.

Today has been a day mostly of contentment and little striving to grab the next rung. That feels good!

WEDNESDAY, NOVEMBER 26TH

Many thanksgivings to and for Christ and His church! Grant, O Lord, in our some small way we might be worthy of both.

Rotary was light in attendance because of it being the day before Thanksgiving. Program was New Castle Boys Basketball coach.

Took time to shop for my wife's birthday gift. Found an ornament that appeared to be just right and bought it.

Spent more time than usual pondering the future. Recognized the power of others to shape it. Being individualistic, this has been a hard thing for me to accept. God is God and yet He allows and enables others to influence us, sometimes far more than we realize in our early years.

"Lead kindly light," as John Henry Cardinal Newman says, into the depths and riches of the Christian Faith.

THURSDAY, NOVEMBER 27TH

How good it is, O Lord, another Thanksgiving Day has come! It is a precious day for all peoples and religions.

This is my wife's birthday. She is sixty-eight years of age. There have been times when both of us thought she would not live that long!

Our family came to an overflowing table of food. When I gave thanks, we all held hands together—including the grandchildren. What a blessing! Having begun that little ritual with Natalie several months ago, Martha, and Jeff are mostly responsible for this. Just to be happily together with God's presence means more than words can convey. Believe Anne Marie was spiritually present.

Remember visiting Thanksgiving Square in Dallas, during a Jewish-Christian National Workshop in 1983. Visited at length with Sister Lois Bannon and many others.

Teach us, God, to give our sorrows and failures, joys, and successes to You in thanksgiving for Your undying presence among us.

FRIDAY, NOVEMBER 28TH

Keep my family and me ever safe in Your everlasting arms, O God. Giving thanks for countless people. How can I ever name them all!

There were Helen Stone (typist), Isabel Boyer (*Indianapolis Star*), Ruth Braselton (Presbyterian laywoman), Bob Koenig (UMC pastor), David Rees (lawyer), and Jeff Gros (RC ecumenist).

Add to them Virginia Gale (WGN Chicago radio), Gary Reif (Associate), Mark Eutsler (Associate), Father Richard Bradford (RC priest), and Julie Largent (book distributor).

Then, how can I forget Ellen Shockey (CSS Publishing), Father Peter Stravinskas (RC editor), Darrel Radford (editor), Nancy Baxter (editor), and Ray Waddle (*Interpreter* magazine).

There are so many to thank, Lord. Please, during this year of reflection, if I forget someone, forgive me!

SATURDAY, NOVEMBER 29TH

The most precious and valuable thing in this world and the next is to be a redeemed son of the living God.

Went to Plainfield to do a book signing at the Family Christian Book Store. New manager, Jeff, was gracious and efficient. Sales were sluggish at first and then by early evening they were really good. Sold eight books in less than an hour, which was excellent for me. Left the store with enthusiasm and sensed the success of God's gift. He prodded me to stay until the numbers came!

Return home was one of joy. Big chef salad at Bob Evans provided tasty respite on the way back to Muncie.

Will the United Methodist Church continue to seek saving itself as a separate and distinct denomination and in the process fail to lose itself as a significant component in the one, holy, catholic, apostolic church? The strong emphasis on Wesleyan theology and doctrine poses a threat to the broader picture of Christian Unity. We need to pray about this!

If we walk in the light as He is in the light, we have fellowship with one another.

SUNDAY, NOVEMBER 30TH

Ice and snow this morning. Older men need to be careful. Thank You, Lord, for allowing me to get older!

We worshipped at First Presbyterian Church in New Castle. Pastor Rex Espiritu is a brilliant fellow! Strong biblical basis in his preaching and a fearlessness in his style. He has been my guest on different occasions at Rotary.

We ate at the new Bella Vita restaurant. This is an investment for a former parishioner at Seymour First UMC, namely Tim Durham. He was a teenager at the time. The decor and meals were impressive. Business will likely come from a wide area.

Even though I reside in Muncie, I spend much time in New Castle and like it that way! After all, I was born in Henry County.

Thank You, Lord, for the assurance I am a child of God. I do not know the day or hour I will die, but I certainly want to be ready.

DECEMBER
2 0 0 8

MONDAY, DECEMBER 1ST

Praise be to You, O God, for the truly good people among us. As I converse with those I have never seen before, I am amazed!

Spent the morning mostly on the computer and Internet. Thank You, Lord, for the skills I have been able to develop.

Ran errands to the bank, post office, etc. Delightful to go several places and almost always know someone.

Received heartwarming letter from an old friend Ron Yonker living in South Carolina. He is an inspiring ecumenist and loves the Lord!

Lord Jesus, keep me ever humble before Your throne that I may walk in Your ways and fulfill my destiny.

TUESDAY, DECEMBER 2ND

Your miracles and mysteries are all about us, God. Thank You for sending a specific person, Jesus the Christ, to be our Savior and Lord.

Read notes from lectures on healing I gave some years ago. Have felt close to this phase of ministry for many years. Our Lord's ministry was really one of preaching, teaching, and healing. Being a chaplain in the International Order of Saint Luke the Physician has been very helpful as a source of information.

Recalled the truly amazing day in 1988 I spent with Father Demetrius Kowalchik OSB at Saint Procopius Abbey in Lisle, Illinois. It was a time of being introduced to the ritual life of the priesthood, plus some really good fellowship with him and others.

My ecumenical orientation to life and ministry has been filled with exciting and blessed events, indeed, far too many to relate in this volume.

Yes, all of life is a gift. Good health and financial resources account, to some extent, for what we do with it. But never underestimate other factors, especially God's surprises!

WEDNESDAY, DECEMBER 3RD

You shall love your God with your whole heart, mind, soul, and strength. You shall also love your neighbor as yourself. Thank You, Lord.

Rotary provided a stimulating time of fellowship. President Kit Crane does an excellent job.

Read old personal journals from the churches at Leesburg, Argos, Walkerton, and Yorktown. They continue to be revealing!

Only You, O Lord, can bring our lives into a meaningful commentary. Indeed, the struggle for wholeness and holiness go together.

It was an evening of light reading, TV, and relaxation. Sometimes, O Lord, I think I am rested up enough!

THURSDAY, DECEMBER 4TH

A baby born in Bethlehem becomes a turning point in the lives of untold numbers. O God, show us how to thank You!

Walked in the Muncie Mall and observed the merchandise offered for sale. Can we ever get away from the lust for more and more?

The media tells us the Anglican Church in North America has been born. Conservatives and traditionalists may soon have their own denomination. Called Bill Ryon in Virginia to get his take on the new group. Called Episcopalians in this area that I know to get their reactions as well. I do believe they are underestimating the new group's potential.

In my experience, the Anglicans (Episcopalians) in this country have sought to be a positive bridge between Roman Catholics and Protestants.

Every time the splinters fly among professing Christians, I am reminded: how shall we escape if we neglect so great a salvation?

FRIDAY, DECEMBER 5TH

Praise God, from Whom all life begins and flows. Praise Him for His Son, Jesus the Christ, Who is our Savior and Lord.

Walked in the Muncie Mall and noted Books-A-Million had a fresh supply of my *Fast Food for the Soul*. Pleased by that!

Went to Christmas party for the Muncie UMC District clergy and their spouses at Welliver's in Hagerstown, Indiana. We sat with Mark Ellcessor and his wife. He is pastor of Selma UMC, east of Muncie. Likeable couple. Also visited with Jason Morris, a young pastor, and his wife. Jason is a very talented fellow and was briefly on the staff during my time at Yorktown UMC.

Clergy gatherings with spouses can be quite satisfying, but also a bit depressing! For the most part, I have found them satisfying and in some cases inspiring.

I have never viewed retirement as inhibiting ministry, but an experience that provides more flexibility in terms of potential growth.

SATURDAY, DECEMBER 6TH

Unto You, O God, I give myself again and again. My only real and ever-lasting hope is in You.

Headed for Barnes and Noble in Bloomington to do a book signing. Treacherous driving in places with both snow and ice. Flow of people at Barnes and Noble was limited. Michelle, as always, was good to promote my books and kind in her approach. Meaningful conversations, especially with women. Not all of them bought books, but there was solid interest in my ministry.

Prayed for God's protection during such inclement weather. I have grown quite dependent on the dear Lord!

Recalled an incident during my undergraduate days at Ball State that still makes me shudder. It was during my first year and I became ill with a temperature of 107 degrees of fever. I was at my home in a rural area and we had no telephone. My father drove to a neighbor's house to call and summoned a physician to my rescue.

Can we ever thank God enough for our blessings? I don't think so, but we can live in an attitude of gratitude.

SUNDAY, DECEMBER 7TH

Remind us, O Lord, of Your mercies on this Pearl Harbor Day. For the USA, the Second World War had begun and victory for us would not come soon. On that fateful day in 1941, which was also a Sunday, I was a slim little boy almost nine years of age and my brother Joseph Allen was nearly three. We lived in the small Henry County (Indiana) town of Blountsville, across from the grain elevator. My father and his friend Kenneth Parks listened intently to the radio.

Today we worshipped at Saint Andrew Presbyterian. The music, especially the harpist, was excellent.

I signed books at the local Muncie Mall Books-A-Million store. It went quite well and I met one lady for whom I had performed her wedding.

How great God is and yet how important and even special we must be to Him. Yes, we are called to give thanks.

It was a satisfying day filled with many enjoyable experiences. God is responsible for this, but He is also responsible for days not so satisfying that may be even more beneficial to us in the long run!

MONDAY, DECEMBER 8TH

O Lord, how can I thank all of the people who have come into my life and enriched it? Thank You.

A day mostly getting Christmas letters ready for mailing. I was able to mail many of them.

How does one know where to start and stop in selecting persons to receive mailings? The potential has always seemed unlimited!

The appointment to Yorktown UMC in 1999 opened the door to many persons—past, present, and future.

It was a work of the Holy Spirit to bring me back for my final appointment to an area where I was born, grew up, went to college, and taught school.

TUESDAY, DECEMBER 9TH

Almighty and ever-living God, how good it is to be part of Your creation. Even better, how good it is to be saved by the precious blood of Your Son!

Ongoing work on the computer with different projects and interests at work. Thank You, Lord, for opportunities galore.

News broke that the governor of Illinois was attempting to sell President-elect Obama's senate seat. May God be merciful to all of us!

The reality and stench of politics in Illinois, especially in Chicago, was communicated to me by Uncle Hopkins Kleihaur, UMC pastor, sixty years ago!

Enjoyable day with Dorothy. We are having more quality time together and that is a big plus!

WEDNESDAY, DECEMBER 10TH

Help us, O Lord, to pour out our hearts to You, not only in repentance, but in thanksgiving as well.

Continue to teach me, Holy Spirit. After all these years, I am learning some things new and much needed.

Keith Kincaid, new pastor of First Christian Church (Disciples of Christ), was my guest speaker and program at Rotary. Keith is a former attorney. I knew former pastors Bob Stauffer and Dave Livingstone there.

Picked up Justin Daniel's birthday gift. It's his first one and I want it to be special. I am so grateful he is a healthy little fellow. Thank You, Lord, for my grandchildren.

A relaxing evening with dinner out and pleasant conversation. Sometimes my wife and I can be like a couple of little kids!

THURSDAY, DECEMBER 11TH

The angels are singing in the heavens in anticipation of the Christ Child, born of the Blessed Virgin Mary.

Help us, heavenly Father, to prepare intently for the birth of the Babe born in Bethlehem. We celebrate this one-of-a-kind event.

A day mostly of preparing and sending Christmas greetings. I have always enjoyed doing this and frequently find it inspirational. I must confess, I avoid the secular Santa Claus and the feel good stuff devoid of the emphasis on the Christ.

A Mother and Her Infant Son has been a favorite for more than twenty years. At one point in time, it was a best seller of mine for CSS Publishing. It was originally published as *A Mother's Questions*.

Dear God, please give us a wondrous Christmas with a perfect blend of repentance, joy, and love.

FRIDAY, DECEMBER 12TH

Almighty God, keep me humble and obedient to the Holy Spirit, like the apostles of old. Love me and purge me of all impurities.

Donna and Terry's wedding anniversary is today. They were married at Saint Luke's UMC in Indianapolis. I assisted Bob Epps and gave them their wedding vows. The soloist was magnificent!

Went to Greenwood to do book signing at Walden's. Considering the mood of the people, the sales were good. Aggressive salesmanship on my part sold some copies! Last book I signed was *Collected Works*, bought by a lovely young woman who had UMC ministers in her family.

This is Justin Daniel's first birthday. His older sister, Natalie Rene, wanted a baby sister and said so, but I guess she will have to adjust anyway!

Well, yes, I really did not want to retire, but so many growth experiences have come about since June of 2003, I really cannot complain. Wherever you are, ministry can always be done.

SATURDAY, DECEMBER 13TH

How precious is Your presence, O Lord. You walk with me and talk with me, telling me I am Your own.

Left early for Terre Haute. Sitting in Bob Evans in that city at 9:00 AM! Traffic light and highways dry.

Open Door Christian Store was very impressive! Had not been there before. Flow of people was great and so were sales. The staff cared that I was there and responded in ways that I truly appreciated. The Red Hat Society was having their luncheon and meeting there; this was helpful. All in all, it was a fun time.

Trip home was quick and accident-free. Gave thanks to God for motoring all those miles in safety and comfort.

The Christian Faith continues among us, victoriously and mysteriously, in both spoken and unspoken ways. Who knows what life in that bookstore has been touched this day that will bear fruit years from now?

SUNDAY, DECEMBER 14TH

Divine and holy love came down at Christmas. We are called to know this Christ Child much better and more completely.

Worshipped at High Street UMC in Muncie. It was a very moving experience. There was an orchestra, Crucifer, and Advent candle-lighting. The entire service made for an atmosphere of worshipping in a European Cathedral. We were blessed with culture, sophistication, and the Holy Spirit!

Did a signing at Books-A-Million in Muncie Mall. Lance and Mary Jo Estep from Yorktown UMC came by, visited, and bought a signed copy.

My place in the community seems to be getting larger. I don't really know what that means, but I will take it as a walk in faith. Dear Lord, I want only what You want!

In a way, Advent is a winter Lent and seeks to prepare us for celebrating the birth of our Savior and Lord.

MONDAY, DECEMBER 15TH

Holy God, forgive us all our sins and restore us to Your Kingdom. I beg of You to cause the United States of America to repent in all seriousness and humility.

Worked on my Associates newsletter. Some of them have enriched my life profoundly and I deeply appreciate it.

Continued to send Christmas letters to others. Wouldn't it be a wonderful thing to pull everyone you have known together and thank them? I believe through our prayers, such persons, living or dead, can sense our thoughts and feelings.

In my long career, I have encountered few enemies, at least, that I know about. To them I say you are forgiven and I do so knowing full well this is only by the Grace of God.

During my emotional upheavals, the Lord stays close and points to better days with Him and others. Let us put away all fakery and become humble boys and girls looking hopefully to their heavenly Father.

TUESDAY, DECEMBER 16TH

I love Your Kingdom, Lord, both the visible and invisible Church. Please keep all professing Christians alert to both.

Christmas greetings are beginning to flow into our household. All are welcome and we celebrate their coming.

Want to stay in contact with all the churches I served. They were all gifts from God and I give thanks.

The dear Lord continues to teach me. Yes, there are some things I need to learn before I die!

O Lord, please deal with my relatives, who seem to be so far from You. Cause them to come to You with open minds and hearts.

WEDNESDAY, DECEMBER 17TH

How marvelous and mysterious are Your miracles, O Lord! I guess we shall understand by and by.

Led by the Holy Spirit to Bob Evans restaurant in Muncie. While there, a waitress in tears asked me to pray for her and her mother. I did, there and then.

Sometimes the wars between the Holy Spirit and the evil one are so real, one can sense the power of them in conflict. Saint Paul understood this very well and we must read him often for our own spiritual upbuilding.

Rotary meeting had some sadness to it. The president, Kit Crane, announced he would be going on active duty with the National Guard at the end of the year. Phil King becomes acting president.

Hold me tightly, Lord, that I might not wander away from Your leading. It sometimes seems so easy to plunge ahead, alone in frustration, with the best of intentions, but not in harmony with the Holy Spirit.

THURSDAY, DECEMBER 18TH

O Father, we beg of You to revive Your people. Our nation needs serious and continual Christian witnessing above everything else.

The media may or may not mislead us, Lord. If we stay humbly and sincerely with You, we are safe in all our dealings with others.

Gave thanks for the good people I meet everyday. I have discovered one of the best places to do this is in restaurants, far and wide. Alert waiters and waitresses can add much to these relationships. There is an art to treating people well and everyone usually needs affirmation. Yes, and remember to be generous with your tips!

Spent much of the day working with Christmas greetings from Catholic institutions to be sent to others. Believe this is a genuinely helpful ministry and the Holy Spirit accomplishes much.

If my Catholic friends—along with millions of Protestants and Orthodox—would practice daily their Faith wholeheartedly, the world would greatly change for the better. Help us, Lord, help us!

FRIDAY, DECEMBER 19TH

Winter has come to our part of the country with snow, ice, and sleet. The driving is treacherous; be with us, Lord.

Motored to Kokomo to do signing for Books-A-Million. Daryl was ready for me with table and books in place. One tall, and stately-like lady bought five copies of my books. I was thrilled and gave thanks to our generous God. Mall and parking lot were very crowded. Sales were quite good, so I left on time, a happy camper.

When I arrived home, I looked at the new Christmas photo of our grand-children Natalie Rene and Justin Daniel. It was an inspirational treasure!

Our emotions can play tricks on us and we can be unaware, becoming confused. Only God, Who knows all, can help us with this sometimes hurtful and occasionally tragic condition.

Recalled the time my great grandfather Charles McCall died. I was twelve years of age. My father cried with deep regret and lamented he had not talked to his grandfather about his soul.

SATURDAY, DECEMBER 20TH

Thank You, Lord, for everything and everyone. Grant Your will be done and Your ways prevail, especially in the president of the United States.

Trip to Indianapolis for signing was enjoyable. Traveling East 86th Street, in particular, was a time of reminiscing. I passed Union Chapel UMC, where I served from 1970 to 1973. The church offered so much in potential, but has never realized it.

There was a mix-up at Books-A-Million because the manager had resigned and neglected to tell them I was coming! However, all seemed to turn out well with me providing the books. The interim manager worked hard to salvage the situation and was mostly successful. As we visited about places I had pastored churches, conversations became very interesting. This was especially true of Hagerstown, Indiana. Yes, it is a small world!

Economic times are uncertain and what has worked to make us happy in other times no longer does so. On the horizon, we see God's patience becoming exhausted and judgment coming to the forefront.

I have read the Holy Scriptures all my life and still wonder about seemingly simple passages in the New Testament. Insights, Lord, insights!

SUNDAY, DECEMBER 21ST

Prepare us for a special day, great God. Our twelve-year-old grandson, Fillip A. L. Beyl, is being baptized at Saint Luke's UMC in Indianapolis.

Our family gathered for the 11:00 AM worship service. We sat together as a family and cherished having our little Grahams, Natalie Rene and Justin Daniel, with us. After the service, we had a private baptism for Fillip. Dr. M. Kent Millard did the officiating.

After the ceremony, we gathered together at The Hawthorns Country Club in Fishers for brunch. This was courtesy of Donna and Terry Beyl.

My father and mother were baptized by immersion in a river. While I respect that form, I believe other ways are equally legitimate.

Dorothy was going to an entertainment with Donna, Sharon, and Martha, so I came home alone. It was bitterly cold with below zero wind chill factor.

MONDAY, DECEMBER 22ND

Thanksgiving is in order, Lord, and more than that, it needs to be a way of life! Saint Paul's Letters tell us over and over to be thankful.

More bitter cold. I must admit, such weather is invigorating and makes me move about more rapidly. The old guy needs to stay active, honoring his body's needs!

Took time to do some Christmas shopping for son-in-law Terry Beyl. He wants Indiana University and Indianapolis Colts wearing apparel. I complied with both.

Interesting and sometimes provocative conversations in Maxwell's Barbershop and 12th Street Café here in Muncie. Church and/or religion invariably enters. I do my best just to listen and that takes a lot of self-discipline! There certainly is an individualism that enters into the picture, loud and clear. My growing up was in this type of environment, so I usually know what to expect.

The celebration of the birth of Jesus the Christ is near. Help all of us, Lord, to experience more of the depths of our Faith. Generally, we want only the veneer and little more.

TUESDAY, DECEMBER 23RD

Our eternal souls, O God, belong to You. To spend eternity with You is our focus and goal. We want the bliss promised and depend on Your ever-lasting love.

A morning of walking and shopping in the Muncie Mall. The sales are spectacular! Remind us, Lord, we are not to worry about what we are to eat, drink, and wear. We are to seek the Kingdom of God first.

Continued correspondence on the national level, especially with ecumenical relevance. This activity has been a fascinating part of my ministry for many years, regardless of the church I am pastoring. I count it a privilege that others far better known than I take the time to correspond.

Ice storm came through central Indiana and paralyzed us for a time. Numerous accidents and some deaths resulted.

Soberly continued to reflect on the past, present, and future. Predestination has often been a part of my thinking. Only God has the truth to that term. Paradoxes are much with us. Yet, for me, they only enhance my belief that God's plan for me was set in motion long ago and continually is fulfilled according to His will. I succumb with full trust in Him.

WEDNESDAY, DECEMBER 24TH

Holy Father, thank You for another Christmas Eve, especially the many times I presided at worship services. There were so many inspirational and beautiful ones! Those with Holy Communion were always the most fulfilling.

Went to the Bureau of Motor Vehicles locally and got my driver's license. Struck by the fact I was the only one in there being served.

Able to pick up Christmas cards for my grandchildren's gifts. Promptly wrote checks and placed them into cards for our tree. I was sixty-three years old before my first grandchild, Fillip, was born. He is a fine lad, well-groomed and well-behaved.

Heavy with a cold, so I spent most of the afternoon snoozing. That was a rarity for me and, frankly, I don't like doing it! Felt much better afterward.

Quiet evening with some TV, reading Christmas letters sent to us, and pondering the future. How good it is to be a part of the Family of God!

THURSDAY, DECEMBER 25TH

Today we celebrate the birth of Jesus the Christ. To argue for or against this being the exact day of his birth is irrelevant. No other birth has so influenced humanity. He comes promising a new way of living. If we Christians are sincere and humbly obedient, we know the truth expounded.

As a change of pace, I took Dorothy to IHOP for breakfast. It was a first for us on Christmas Day. It was good for both of us.

Wrote a letter or two. I also sorted through journals and files again. They have been helpful in doing this autobiography.

Went through some of Anne Marie's folders and tended to relive the tragedy of her death. In her teens, she was a lovely and very intelligent young woman. I suppose we all want to lock our children into a certain age and time, leaving them there!

Ended the day somewhat frustrated but, as always, thankful and confident in God's ever-present grace.

FRIDAY, DECEMBER 26TH

Our Faith teaches us there is one God in three persons: Father, Son, and Holy Spirit. The reality and mystery of the Trinity is ours to accept.

Spent time looking at two major reform movements: Forward in Faith and the Confessing Movement. The first is basically Anglican and seeks to restore biblical authority. The second claims to be within the United Methodist Church and seeks to do the same. Both tend to be disruptive.

Yet, how can God's errant people be brought back to their roots and purified? I find strength in both of them and believe their core purpose is inspired and justified.

All-wise God, we plead with You to keep us humble before Your Son's cross. Forgive our wayward ways that destroy our witness to a lost and dying world.

In the parishes, I always found the days after Christmas and before the New Year to be excellent, uninterrupted working times. They allowed for prolonged concentration on whatever needed to be done.

We clergy are called to keep digging deeper and deeper in the riches of our Faith. We cannot really afford to be completely satisfied with our walk with Christ.

SATURDAY, DECEMBER 27TH

Thank You, Father, for this life and the hope to come. Your assurances are always with me. What would I do without them?

Visited with a man at Mac's Muncie restaurant. Having visited with him before, I saw him in a particular way. Come to find out, his wife has been an invalid for many years. That changed my view of him. A spiritual growth moment for me!

Our family began arriving just before noon. It is our Christmas family celebration. My wife worked so hard getting ready for it. The food, gifts, and relationships were inspiring. Thank you, dear Lord.

Love is patient and kind; it is not jealous or boastful. Yes, Lord, I hear You through Your servant, Saint Paul.

So much more to learn and appreciate. Grant, Lord, I would never lose the capacity and desire for both.

SUNDAY, DECEMBER 28TH

Began the day with gratitude for my family being present yesterday. It was truly a good day and today will be also!

We went to Fishers UMC for worship. The crowd was slim, but the service was warm and inspiring.

We enjoyed a sumptuous noon meal at Olive Garden near Castleton Mall. Then, we shopped leisurely in the mall.

We also spent some time at Barnes and Noble near there. This was a special treat because we seldom get there.

The trip home was satisfying and we celebrated a day well-spent. Praise God from Whom all blessings flow, praise Him all creatures here below.

MONDAY, DECEMBER 29TH

Love is our paramount gift and virtue. It is best illustrated by the crucifixion of our Savior, Jesus the Christ.

Paid end-of-the-month bills and finished my column for the *Star Press* (Muncie). Delighted to have the money to pay all our bills and begin another year writing for the paper.

Made plans to visit a waitress's mother at a trailer park. The waitress works at Bob Evans. She does good ministry among those who appreciate her kindness and authenticity. Arrived about 2:00 PM and visited about an hour. Her mother has health problems and needed spiritual comfort. She was very appreciate of my visit.

For many years, I have thought churches and denominations should underwrite persons who would simply visit places, especially restaurants, and become available for whatever needs are to be met. There is so much need out there! This would take a great spiritual heart, resiliency and flexibility. Such a person must be rooted and grounded in the Christian Faith. Last, but not least, it would take someone with a strong sense of accountability.

It was a uniquely different day and I was privileged to serve those with little earthly goods and illness.

TUESDAY, DECEMBER 30TH

Someone needs You, Lord; come by here. We always need You, Lord, sometimes more so than others! Yes, we are a needy people.

Walked in the Muncie Mall for about an hour. People come and go. Each and everyone has a story to tell and needs another person(s) to listen.

Worked in my study. Attempted to sort out the past, present, and future. I belong to You, Lord! Do with me what You will.

Nearing the end of another year and I will soon be seventy-six years of age. Nationally, it has been troublesome and, at times, frightening.

Transitions come and go, but now we are living in a time of major and far-reaching change. God's patience with us appears to have reached its limits. Judgment has come, but it is not an end within itself. Holy and everlasting God, I beg of You to be with the United States of America.

Lord, please remember my brother Mike, who is having some health problems. Be ever near him and his wife, Alecia.

WEDNESDAY, DECEMBER 31ST

O Lord, how good You are to me. Day and night, night and day, You are with me. What more can I ask?

Ate lunch at the Muncie Olive Garden with Jim MacDougall (Roman Catholic) and Jim Beckley (UMC). It was a nourishing time! MacDougall is a permanent deacon and a Christian gentleman throughout with a love for prison ministry. Beckley spent most of his career as a military chaplain with much of it occurring outside of the United States.

Remind me, Lord, with my pastoral style, I tend to greet every stranger like a long-lost friend. This is especially true at book signing events. Some persons are not ready for that and react with rejection. I am called to be not only considerate, but lovingly patient.

Even in my seventy-fifth year, I have been taught many significant things, Lord. You are a marvelous Rabbi! Keep me teachable.

As the door closes on 2008, I give thanks to the God Who created me. I view the future with God-given optimism and hope. Very grateful His Son will never leave me or forsake me.

INDEX

ABOUT THE AUTHOR

Born in Henry County, Indiana between New Castle and Muncie, Donald Charles Lacy went to elementary school in Blountsville and graduated from Center High School (Wapahani) in Perry Township of Delaware County.

His early professional background was in teaching social studies and English in Redkey and Dunkirk schools of Jay County, Indiana.

As a pastor for more than fifty years in the United Methodist Church, Lacy has served in a variety of localities. His churches have been across the state of Indiana.

As a writer, he began in 1960 and has continued this ministry. It has resulted in his fifteenth book, along with numerous newspaper columns and magazine features.

As a leader in Christian Unity and interreligious dialogue, Lacy has ministered at local, state, and national levels. *Time* magazine interviewed him in its March 21, 2005 issue.

As a community leader and participant, Lacy has been president of both Lions and Rotary clubs. Among his many memberships have been Scottish Rite (Indianapolis), York Rite College (Fort Wayne), and Phi Delta Kappa.

Dr. Lacy is a graduate of Ball State University (BS & MA) and Christian Theological Seminary (MDIV & DMIN).

His work is being placed in the Indiana Historical Society, Christian Theological Seminary, and DePauw University.